he's not t

she's not the enemy,

and neither is HE

Suffering: the Good, the Bad, and the Joyful

MARCIA RAE ESCOBAR

Foreword by Pastor Mark Mann

he's not the enemy, she's not the enemy, and neither is HE

Trilogy Christian Publishers
A Wholly Owned Subsidiary of Trinity Broadcasting Network
2442 Michelle Drive, Tustin, CA 92780

Copyright © 2024 by Marcia Rae Escobar

Scripture quotations marked ESV are taken from the English Standard Version. Copyright © 2001 by Crossway, a publishing ministry of Good News Publishers. Used by permission. All rights reserved.

Scripture quotations marked KJV are taken from the King James Version®. Public domain.

Scripture quotations marked NIV are taken from the New International Version. Copyright © 1973, 1978, 1984, 2011 by Biblica, Inc®. Used by permission. All rights reserved worldwide.

Scripture quotations marked NKJV are taken from the New King James Version®. Copyright © 1990 by Thomas Nelson. Used by permission. All rights reserved.

Scripture quotations marked NASB are taken from the (NASB®) New American Standard Bible®, Copyright © 1960, 1971, 1977, 1995, 2020 by The Lockman Foundation. Used by permission. All rights reserved. www.lockman.org.

All rights reserved, including the right to reproduce this book or portions thereof in any form whatsoever. For information, address Trilogy Christian Publishing Rights Department, 2442 Michelle Drive, Tustin, CA 92780.

Trilogy Christian Publishing/ TBN and colophon are trademarks of Trinity Broadcasting Network.

For information about special discounts for bulk purchases, please contact Trilogy Christian Publishing.

Trilogy Disclaimer: The views and content expressed in this book are those of the author and may not necessarily reflect the views and doctrine of Trilogy Christian Publishing or the Trinity Broadcasting Network.

10 9 8 7 6 5 4 3 2 1

Library of Congress Cataloging-in-Publication Data is available.

ISBN 979-8-89597-150-5
ISBN 979-8-89597-151-2 (ebook)

DEDICATION

I dedicate this book to my husband and our three adult children, who have all walked through this journey out of the woods with me. You have seen me at my ugliest, and at times, it took everything in you to continue to love me. I knew you longed for a wife and mom who could handle the throes of life. Having grown up with the example of shame, anger, hostility, negativity, and hatred, these were the ways that I learned from an early age and continued to walk in them without showing you a good and godly example in suffering well for the glory of God. You have walked with me knowing my stories of abuse, misuse, infidelity, health, and death issues. God has been faithful in all of this to teach me that *he's not the enemy, she's not the enemy, and neither is HE.*

My dear family, I thank you for hanging in there with me, watching me do it all wrong, for forgiving me for not setting the right example, and for coming back to the right form of love with me. I do not take this love lightly, and I thank God for each of you and our sweet grandchildren and all your wonderful God-given mates for life. You all are amazing in your growth in spite of my example. I love you all forever and always, and pray that my heavenly Father will bless your families with the right representations of His love, showing you that His ways are far above our ways. I long for this for each of you.

To my friend and pilgrim, Terri. This book would not be complete without you. I thank you for teaching me about the grace of God and his forgiveness. Thank you for loving me so well with God's truth. You taught me that shame is not God's method but forgiveness is. You wrapped your arms around me by giving me God's Word like no one to that point in my life had ever done. The Word of God became alive to me, and I surrendered to Him in salvation as a result of your care and love at one of the most awful times of my life. You knew my family, and we had attended the same school and church for a short time together, and God placed you back in my life, in His providence, with the only voice I would trust.

I would also like to dedicate this book to our pastor, Mark Mann, and his wife Barbara. You walked with us when Dan and I were at the worst part of our marriage, and to this day, and have loved us despite our faults. You were faithful to meet us with biblical soul care in the most grievous parts of our marriage, and later in our suffering, our lack of trust, and at times hopelessness, to bring us out of the darkness and offer the best way of living by His grace. We are grateful for your faithful work in the ministry and the impact that this ministry has personally had on us and our family.

To my friend, Kay, and my friend, Jane; there are parts in this book about you as well. Kay, your finding hearts in everything has inspired me to look for and see the best in life and people. Jane, your prayers for me have not gone unnoticed and will resound in my heart forever.

TABLE OF CONTENTS

Dedication iii
Foreword 7
Preface 11
Chapter 1: What We Don't Know Can Hurt Us 13
Chapter 2: Dear Wife with an Aching Soul *(Betrayal,*
    Bitterness, Healing) 25
Chapter 3: Clawing Your Way to the Top *(Suicidal*
    Ideology and Depression). 41
Chapter 4: Mistrust of a Lifetime 51
Chapter 5: Messing with My Kingdom 65
Chapter 6: A Letter to My Dad *(Unrealistic Imposed*
    Expectations) 71
Chapter 7: Relationships Don't Always Get Healed on
    Earth *(Death)*. 77
Chapter 8: Mama's Shoes *(Legacy)* 85
Chapter 9: Take Me to the Temple *(Missing Out on Life)* . 89
Chapter 10: Living by Faith in the "In-Between" of
    Chronic Illness 93
Chapter 11: Running Knees—the Power of God's
    Word and Prayer 97
Chapter 12: Running Knees—Intercession *(Letting*
    People In) 105
Chapter 13: Finding Hearts Everywhere *(Looking with*
    Spirit Eyes) 107
Chapter 14: Becoming Sparkly *(Where Do You Find*
    Comfort?) 109

FOREWORD

Life in this fallen world is fraught with difficulties, struggles, and tragedies. But God assures Christians that our sufferings are much more than random or pointless; they serve an eternal purpose (Romans 8:28–29). Those who endure suffering at the hands of others, especially loved and trusted family members, are afflicted with particularly deep wounds that scar their hearts and predispose them to aberrant behavior themselves.

Marcia Escobar presents us with a realistic, gritty, often disturbing account of her own life experiences. In just fifty-two pages, she presents both a bird's eye view of her life, while occasionally dropping down to give us a worms-eye view of the ugliness of the sin she was exposed to. Most people live their whole life without experiencing childhood sexual abuse, ongoing verbal and mental abuse from a parent, or the betrayal of an adulterous spouse. Marcia experienced them all.

Woven into the tapestry of her difficult life is the ever-present God she had come to know, to love, and to trust; a Savior whom she would learn had been with her all through her turbulent life. But the journey was never easy. In fact, her sufferings would, at times, wear her down to the point that her faith in God became threadbare. Even in those dark moments, He was at work—*especially* then.

For it is in our darkest hours of suffering that God uses the fiery pain we experience to burn away the dross from our eyes so we can see God spiritually holding on to our vision of Him like a lifeline, looking to Him, trusting Him, finding hope in Him, receiving crucial life-sustaining grace from Him. This is Marcia's story.

> *For you, O God, have tested us; you have tried us as silver is tried. You brought us into the net; you laid a crushing burden on our backs; you let men ride over our heads; we went through fire and through water; yet you have brought us out to a place of abundance.*
>
> — Psalm 66:10–12 (ESV)

Marcia chronicles an entire lifetime of troubling events that are often painful to read. Her pain is real. Her story is visceral. But the hope of the gospel and God's deliverance is the scarlet thread that runs through her entire story. All to the glory of God!

Read her story. Find yourself in it and take courage while gaining confidence that God's Word is a sufficient source of encouragement since it is God speaking life transforming truth into our hearts to dispel the lies that sought to defeat us, and to reconcile the sins that would otherwise conquer us. Marcia's compelling narrative invites all who read to come to know the Savior who supplies the truths that will set you free (John 8:31–32; 2 Corinthians 10:3–5).

> *When you pass through the waters, I will be with you; and through the rivers, they shall not overwhelm you; when you walk through fire you shall not be burned,*

and the flame shall not consume you. For I am the LORD your God, the Holy One of Israel, your Savior.

— Isaiah 43:2–3 (ESV)

This is God's promise to all those who turn to Him for help.

— Pastor Mark Mann
Grace Bible Fellowship
Mt. Juliet, Tennessee

PREFACE

I do not pretend to have all the answers for suffering in this Christian walk, but I have met and have become the child of the ONE who does. It is by the grace of my Savior, Jesus Christ, that I bring this book to you, sharing small portions of my life with you. As I have traversed the strangling weeds of being lost in the woods of my life, HE is the ONE who brought me out of the woods into His wonderful and boundless rippling brook and glorious waterfall of His glorious grace.

This book has been written with you in mind so that you will know that you are not alone. There are countless who have struggled with mental health, betrayal, death, abuse, and expectations of others, have been caught up in shame, and have felt hopeless. It is my prayer that as you read this book, that God will meet you with His Word and not merely with my words, to offer hope and a way out of the dark shadows of the woods and into the rapturous light of His boundless love.

I suggest that you have your Bible app or your Bible handy as you read this book as God has given me many verses to share with you as a help as you read.

CHAPTER 1

What We Don't Know Can Hurt Us

> *Your eyes saw my unformed substance; in your book were written, every one of them, the days that were formed for me, when as yet there was none of them.*
>
> — Psalm 139:16 (ESV)

No one likes to be kept in the dark, and especially regarding topics that directly involve them and their lives.

I am talking about a need to know *everything*. I am speaking of the digging and endless searching, the gossip and recruitment to a cause, to find out what we can about people whom we sinfully desire to destroy since they have so maliciously "destroyed" us and have seemingly "gotten away with" their destruction. It is a desire to have all knowledge and to inspect and decide in your mind and heart what you will do with that information. It could be "the other woman," "the other man," the nosey neighbor, the cruel boss, the distant or hateful family member, or a multitude of other people in your life. I'm sure the possibilities are endless, and this is not a book about getting your pound of flesh. It is instead, a book of warning and praising God for what He alone can do with a heart dedicated to Him.

Allow me to digress.

When I was a young girl, I grew up on the land. My folks made sure we always had land on which to play and to work. And play I did as a little girl! Oh, what fun I had climbing the cherry and plum trees, playing hide and seek in the cornfield, swinging and swaying on the tire swing, ice skating on the creek wearing my double-bladed, slip-over-the-boot skates, having corn cob fights in the corn crib with my siblings, playing softball in the big front yard until dark with whomever could come from our little farm community. Oh, and yes, through the spring and summer, we worked in our large garden, planting seeds, weeding the garden, picking the vegetables, and preparing them for Mom to can them to put up for our family of seven. Drinking from the water hose outside our old farmhouse was the norm. What I didn't know was that old house and its pipes more than likely had toxic lead.

We lived on that beloved farm until I was nine years old. There were secret things that happened on that farm that ate me up on the inside until I got help from my pastor to finally lay these secrets at Jesus' feet while in my fifties. What I did not share and what my parents did not know was hurting me and confusing them.

When I was nine, we moved for a brief time to a home that didn't have as much land, and my siblings and I always found more land. Whether it was in going on miles-long bike rides out in the country or walking to a little corner (most likely about an acre) slice of woods where we would have endless adventures playing in the woods or walking down the road to fish in the pond. We always wanted and found the land.

After living in this little neighborhood for five years, we moved to a house with ten lovely acres of land again, having a creek, a hillside, room for a garden, and beloved woods, beautiful sunsets, and ticks. Mom would burn the butts off so many ticks as we kids brought them in on us, not having a clue of the danger in those little varmints.

When I was a teenager, I continued to spend time in the woods, mainly just to walk and think and dream and wish that I did not have any secrets in my life. I talked to God in those woods, and I longed for Him to speak to me. I had no doubt that He knew who I was, but boy, I sure did not feel like He could possibly love me. In those woods and in my bed each night, I would ask for God's forgiveness and ask Him to save me every night. I didn't know that He wanted all of me in true repentance. I had shameful secrets, and those secrets compounded on each other with new sinful activities.

Little did I know that the explorations of my childhood days had excited a passion within me that was way before its time. These secrets drove me to rage on many occasions, most often directed at my mom, as Dad would never have allowed these outbursts, even though he was the master of outbursts. I did not know what to do with the jumbled-up mess in my head and in my heart.

So, what I didn't know *did* hurt me. It did hurt my parents, even unwittingly. These pains drove a wedge in our relationship for many years. I didn't know what to do with that. All I knew was that I didn't feel protected from people who would hurt that cute little blonde girl. I did not share my life with my parents in conversation as I started my teen years. These secrets drove a wedge that created much more distrust and seemingly no way out of these shameful secrets.

As a sophomore in high school, I almost told my teacher about my secrets as she told me that I could spend time with God in the Bible, and I could write things out to Him. And so began my love for writing and communing with God. I had walked the aisle as a six-year-old at church, but that is all I remembered as I continued my life of nightly confessions to the ceiling of my bedroom. I tried to read the Bible, and nothing made sense to me for the longest time. This was truly all about me and in no way about Jesus. I have learned since that I was only used to complying with the rules and in no way was I free.

I stopped going to the woods so much because one day I had a huge tick on the side of my knee that fell off onto the floor as I was changing, and it left a huge red hole in my leg. We doctored my leg and I went on. What I didn't know did hurt me in my fifties as I was diagnosed with chronic Lyme disease.

After this tick bite in my teenage years, I began to spend a lot more time getting out of the house, filling up my folks' car with gas, visiting friends, and spreading my wings. Little did I know that every time I filled up the car, that I was breathing in toxins from leaded gasolines. I grew up in the sixties, seventies, and eighties. Oh how I loved to just breathe in that smell of gas. I know, silly, but I loved that smell. And I loved the smell of skunks too—ha! Okay, back to the subject. What I didn't know did hurt me with lead poisoning also found in my fifties.

I have learned a lot in my fifties that I never knew, never looked for, nor ever put into my health practices to resolve until that time.

While in my twenties, with one child in the womb and a preschooler and a toddler, I found out that what I didn't know could hurt my children when one of our children was sexually molested by a childcare worker in the church we were attending.

I also learned that people don't always want to know what is happening in their families and would rather ignore, burying their heads in the sand so to speak, than to know the truth that their child may also have been molested by the same person. I learned that families should not work together in childcare ministries in churches lest that family is also being molested and abused at home. I learned that the leadership at church does not always go to bat for you in cases like this to confront sin in the church when they should. I learned that even when the legal system has all the proof that is needed to hold a child molester accountable for their actions, they don't always follow the proof that is substantiated by court-ordered child therapy by the state and bring this person to justice. It's a messed-up system for sure.

What we did not know was happening really hurt my family, our church relationship, our faith in the body of believers. We knew that even though the legal system had failed us, that we had biblical grounds to bring this man before the church not only for the sexual harm to our child but also for the harm he was inflicting on his own family. His wife told me while this investigation was going on that she had been severely abused and threatened not to press charges and that all her children had been abused and molested by this man who was their father. I found out that people don't always get held accountable for horrific acts against innocent children and families. We left that church.

I have learned that I used to like to read books from the back to the front, perhaps in some weird subliminal way so that I could know the end and determine if the book would be worth my time or if it would make me too afraid to continue. I learned earlier on in life though that I could watch movies and not be bothered by not seeing the end. Again, maybe because I did not want to see a happy ending because I could not reconcile my life with all its secrets and unaccountability to a "happy" ending.

I learned that I needed Jesus, a relationship that I did not know that I did not have. I had a head full of things I had learned in church but nothing that was personal where I yearned for Christ's answers, where I learned that He had offered forgiveness to me and a plan for me to go through this pain and to come out faithful. What I didn't know did hurt me.

I sought "Christian counseling" that sent me on the path of antidepressants that did not help me to deal with the pain of my child being hurt by another person unbeknownst to me and my husband. It only led me to the need for more and more antidepressants.

I am so thankful that my high school friend, Terri, visited me and asked me why I was thinking that I was owed this pain from God for my own sexual indiscretions in my childhood and teenage years. She shared with me that Christ's grace had already covered me if I was a child of His.

That day, at age twenty-nine, after reading a book she gave to me, along with a book about the cross of Christ, I totally gave my life to Jesus Christ in saving faith. I realized that I then had a hunger and thirst for God's Word like never before. It became clear to me that what I had not understood about Christ was hurting me and leading me directly to the cross for my eternal salvation, sanctification, and a new life.

At the same time, as I was hearing about God's grace for the first time, our new pastor at our new church we were attending was teaching a sermon series entitled, "The Hand of God in the Robbery of Man" about the life of Joseph and the sovereignty of God, yet another truth I had not in any way learned. What I did not know about Christ's sovereignty and my desire to be in control of everything in my life was truly hurting me, crushing me beneath its heavy burden and leading me to suicidal ideologies. When I got into God's Word, and for the first time began to understand what He truly had done for me by the death of His Son on the cross, I saw how my sin was a part of that payment for which Christ had fully paid. What I learned in this truth of Scripture began for the first time to heal me and to give me hope to live, to love, and to care for the needs of my family whom I felt I had failed.

I learned in my forties that if I did not till the garden of my marriage and instead, let the weeds climb in or let the children and ministry become my priority over my marriage, it could hurt the relationship I had with my husband. What I did not know did hurt me and my "ideal" family.

During this busy time of my life, my desire to travel the world the same way I got to as a teenager, with my well-financed parents, crept in. I began working for my dad's roofing business as his administrative assistant. A part of my administrative role was to prepare presentations from the mission trips and for the mission ministry that he and Mom were involved in. I began to travel and that love for overseas travel became more important than my own family. I let a very controlling father and his desire to see his daughter and son-in-law in ministry win over in control of our family. When I wasn't taking a mission trip and teaching women overseas, I was talking about it and became discontented with my life back home. I began to think that my husband and I were called to be overseas missionaries when, in essence, we were Dad-called. He and I were calling the shots, and this was not a calling from God. What my husband didn't know by acquiescing to my desire to be an overseas missionary did hurt me and him and our family. We became unraveled as we began our missionary journey. God was not in this, and He was sure to show us.

When the wheels fell off our marriage due to my husband's adultery shortly after beginning to raise support for this mission endeavor, we saw clearly that what I didn't know did hurt us all tremendously. What I didn't know, but had always felt, was that there was a missing puzzle piece coming to fruition in my marriage. My husband had grown up as a pastor's kid that just went through the motions of Christianity his whole life, and his deceit was catching up with him, and we were all to pay for his years of prior deceit by the full-blown act of his adultery.

What I didn't know was that my desires that I had for living and serving elsewhere in ministry and my discontentment were also a part of this whole pain. Don't hear me say that I was responsible for his adultery, as I was not. In our years of healing from this travesty in our marriage, we have both had to come back to the cross to repent of our parts of the pain in our family, and more than that, the grief this was to our holy God. My husband's repentance after many years of harboring this deceit brought him to true salvation. My need to die daily, and submit to the providential recognition of Christ's not being taken by surprise by any of the events of our marriage and pain in our family, led to my repentance of my control, pride, and bitterness.

Oh, what a journey it has been to walk out, and at times, to just trudge through that repentance.

This is my story, one of fear, discontentment, control, pride, unforgiveness, and a whole world of hurt that kept me stuck in "the woods" of my life, instead of walking beside the still waters of Christ's grace that He had already won for me on the cross.

Some of you will relate to suffering in one way or another as you flip through and read the pages of this book, as you are met with suffering which you can relate to, the expectations of others, people-pleasing, discontentment, the throes of living with chronic illness, and the giving up of hope by elongated suffering. You will relate to child sexual molestation, fear-based parenting you were privy to as a child yourself and that you learned to use in your own parenthood. You will recall sexual misuse of your body at an early age, wishing you were someone else, the heartbreak of an adulterous marriage, and the agony inflicted upon your children which would lead some of your family to even walk away from God as a result. You will find that unforgiveness can lead you to hopelessness to the point of attempted suicide, and that even as you are beginning to walk out of the woods, you may keep going back to what you know. You can more encouragingly find that you are led out of this darkness by that which has been planted deep into your soul by knowing Christ Jesus and His Word. With the Holy Spirit's help, you can relate to tears, anger, bitterness, the joy of finding contentment in Christ, and the defeat of the war with flesh and the spirit (Galatians 5:16–17). You will relate to others not understanding you, and at other times, a judgement of thinking you had your whole life together, and that God let you down as if He owed you a life of ease. You will relate to that embarrassment or people thinking you should be "over" something that is a God-ordained challenge in your life. You may be able to relate to the loss of friends that this shame can bring on you, a shame in which some friends walk away for fear of what they might get on them by staying involved.

My hope is that no matter the hardships that you are enduring, that you will realize that *he's not the enemy; she's not the enemy, and neither is HE*. Perhaps that title should also include "it's not the enemy," but I think you get the point.

I, personally, find it easier to relate to a book that is real; one in which I can find myself and find hope to overcome. I am even more encouraged by those who will take me in a simple way to Scripture to find the hope that I need to live above life's challenges. I am blessed to bless others with the forgiveness which Christ Himself offered to forgive me so freely.

We are put on this Earth with one purpose. That purpose is to glorify God. We do that by our daily walk with Him in Scripture and prayer, our responses to His sovereign times of suffering, and in our sharing with others the hope of the gospel, by meeting them at the cross and speaking words of truth with so much hope. I need this book as much as you do, as a reminder that I am not superior and am humbled to be used by God to bring these truths to you.

CHAPTER 2

Dear Wife with an Aching Soul (Betrayal, Bitterness, Healing)

If I say, "Surely the darkness shall cover me,
 *and the light about me be night," even the darkness
is not dark to you;*
 *the night is bright as the day, for darkness is as
light with you.*

— Psalm 139:11–12 (ESV)

God has allowed me to go through His refining fire in many areas, but there is one area that I would like to share with you today that is more aptly began in story form with headings for effectiveness.

The Dump Heap of Betrayal

Going along, living with my husband and kids, just trying to serve God. And then the news brought dread, fear, anger, sadness, questions too big to answer, with no answer good enough. I felt at that moment that I must be bleeding through my skin. Then bitterness locked in and began to set up housekeeping in my mind, heart, and life.

All these emotions, plus so many more, became the theme of my life until God set me free from them through my obedience. I promise you that this was not an easy obedience, and it took years to truly yield to the Holy Spirit's work in my heart and life. God was always there, and He had everything under control, but how could this be part of His plan? No way!! I loved God, or I thought I did. Did I anymore? How could He allow this?

All I knew is that, suddenly, my husband backed up the dump truck and unloaded all this trash on me and our children with his confession of years of deceit and adultery, and I couldn't see my way to the top, even with Scripture. Those verses that used to give me so much comfort and direction became blurry on the page as that root of bitterness became so strong and hard to break. Try as I might, I couldn't climb to the top or out the sides of this trash heap. I was gasping for air and wanting out of this life. *Go ahead, smother me … it will be easier that way*, began to be the daily coursing thought in my broken heart.

But God … but God says when it is over, not me.

The Housekeeping of Bitterness

A heart that was wallpapered with protection. I would never let this happen again, and he would never do this to me again. I would never be so naive again. I would make sure of that. *Pass the paste, please.*

I couldn't keep the wallpaper from falling when my later repentant husband started loving me and truly showing me this love through his love for pleasing God most of all. And then that was followed up by him not choosing to remain in his sin.

How dare he be forgiven for this! And now I'm supposed to forgive and be okay? An angry heart that spilled forth violent words splattered all over these walls of protection and all over everyone that I loved (Luke 6:45).

Those horrific words and actions were meant to try to hurt him as much as he hurt me, but that was not possible. I couldn't hurt him enough to equal my torment. Yes, misery loves company, but God has a better plan (Hebrews 4:15–16). Christ, our Savior and would-be Lord, has felt the utmost rejection from His heavenly Father as God turned His back on Him and placed the sins of the whole world on Him, including all my ugly sin, not just my husband's sin. *Pass the bleach, please.* I really can't remove the words that I have infectiously sprayed on my home and family. But God can and did (after a longer time than it had to take, if I had chosen to obey). Thank You, Lord.

In the meantime, this wallpaper was not strong enough. I had to reinforce these walls around my heart. Let's see, there's one thing that I wanted more than anything else and that was to have ALL information that I wanted. No, I did not want all the details. By this time, I had received enough of that for a lifetime of hurt, but I should at least be able to get that one last bit of information. Until I got that, I would not be satisfied. This wall of unguarded thoughts remained my last bit of security. And believe me, it is so much stronger than any wallpaper ever was. Two by four and six by eight steel reinforcements are nothing. This was a concrete heart that yields its members as instruments of sin (Romans 6:19–20) and really thinks it has some right to hang onto the hurt that has been inflicted on it. But in hanging onto this lust for my own way (pride), I did forfeit what God had already made available to me ... His grace (read Jonah 2). I knowingly continued in my sin (Romans 6:1–12). Pass another footer, please cuz' I was pouring more concrete in this wall. It was not thick enough to provide safety, nor would it ever be.

Every wall I had placed around my heart was housed in a frame of unforgiveness. I could never forgive this man for doing this to me and my family. We would never be the same. Thank God, I can say now, we will never be the same. You see, God asked me to forgive one person (even seventy times seven times), and God had the whole world to forgive ... even me.

But now the big question: Would I trust God enough to obey Him? (Ephesians 4:32) Would I trust that God had a plan in the deception and sin of my husband that could possibly bring Him glory? Believe me, I didn't want to trust God, but He has shown me who He is repeatedly, and how faithful and how patient and merciful He is as I have now sought Him with all my heart (Matthew 6:33). His grace was sufficient for me, even when I was too weak to believe His plan.

Do You Want to Be Healed? New Walls

The question was asked in my walled-up heart as in the story of the paralytic man wanting to get to the pool of Bethesda when the water was stirring, and Jesus was saying to the man, to me, and to you, "Do you want to be healed?" (John 5:6, ESV). I had already read Jonah 2:8–9. I felt as Jonah did in the stomach of the God-ordained fish that had swallowed him in his disobedient state, that the seaweed of unforgiveness and hatred was strangling me to death and that by clinging to my worthless idols, I was forsaking the grace that could be mine by turning to obedience and the truth that salvation is from the Lord. But when would this freedom be mine?

God was asking me again that same question, "When will you give up on wanting your own way and having to know everything and punishing your husband over and over again?" He was reminding me that my husband was His child. My heavenly Father was challenging me in His Word with my continued questioning of His ways, which are far above my ways (Isaiah 55:8–9).

And as I no longer had any excuses, except for my own pride (Proverbs 16:18), I realized that I had set my life on the course of destruction. And in this destruction, I was setting myself and my family up for destruction, unless God intervened, and of course, He could. I realized this before and surrendered to obey, that through reading Scripture, I would have the Sword of the Spirit to fight this battle and to cast down the imaginations of my heart (2 Corinthians 10:5–6).

So, God has taken down the poorly decorated walls of my heart. He has stripped down that wallpaper of bitterness and replaced it with gladness and trust that He is accomplishing His purposes through, and regardless of, my husband's and my own sins (Romans 8:28–29). He has removed the violent words that would spew forth when I just felt like saying them and replaced them with right and loving and edifying speech (Ephesians 4:29–32). He has replaced my lust for having to know what I wanted to know with wanting to know Him more and to walk in His ways with complete obedience (Ephesians 4:22–24). He has given me the ability to forgive my husband, something which I thought was not possible to truly know and live in. Christ then replaced the fear with peace and true freedom from this and other acts of obedience.

The truth has set me free indeed (John 8:32)! And it is not the truth of what my husband did, nor the truth about my own sin that set me free ... it is the TRUTH OF THE WORD OF GOD (John 17:17)! This means that when I see that verse in Philippians 4:8 that says, *"Finally, brothers, whatever is true, whatever is honorable, whatever is just, whatever is pure, whatever is lovely, whatever is commendable, if there is any excellence, if there is anything worthy of praise, think about these things,"* I don't have to steer away from these promises. I can be tempted to think that there is nothing lovely and true and honest and pure in life anymore. *God is*, and He has become the highest priority in my life, not my husband (although he is a high priority). I now look forward to what God will do with our family as my husband and I strive to trust Him and serve Him faithfully (1 Corinthians 2:9).

My prayer is that these words will comfort you with the comfort with which Christ has comforted me (2 Corinthians 1:3–5) and allow you to see that where sin abounds, grace much more abounds, and that if we confess our sin (the whole of Romans chapter 5), God is faithful and just to forgive us our sin. In the same way He has forgiven my husband's sin of which he has confessed and repented; in the same way as He has forgiven my sin of which I have confessed and repented (1 John 1:9). He has forgiven us wholly of past, present, and future sins, just like He promised. Afford yourself of that same forgiveness and new walk with Christ as all that have bitterness and unforgiveness removed from their lives walk in.

I know that you want affirmation of your pain, and dear sister, I feel your pain, and know it is real, but would ask you to ask yourself, "Do you want to be healed?" Place your hand in the Master Physician's hand and allow Him to soothe your aching soul, and on Him your heavy burdens roll (Matthew 11:28–30). Stay in His Word, and make Him your priority, and we both can say, "Eye has not seen, nor ear heard, nor have entered into the heart of man the things which God has prepared for those who love Him" (1 Corinthians 2:9, NKJV).

May God bless you as, with Christ's help, you remodel your life, your temple of God with His grace and forgiveness, removing the walls of bitterness, fear, control, pride, unforgiveness, and sin (1 Corinthians 6:19–20). He purchased your body, His dwelling place and temple, with the blood of His Son. What a price He paid for my beautification and yours!!! May God be glorified in all we do and say in this process of bringing us back to His image.

....

I have copied all the verses that I have inserted in this story of my condensed journey of my husband's infidelity so that you can look at them, read them aloud, and be comforted and strengthened and challenged. It is God's Word that will give you power. Use it!

The next chapters of this book are formative chapters in my life and not to be avoided as you walk out of, and as I continue to walk out of, the harsh wounds of betrayal and begin to trust God with my life and with others. In my healing, I have learned that, for me, when I read the Word of God out loud, it helps me to understand, comprehend, and apply what I am reading.

> *The good person out of the good treasure of his heart produces good, and the evil person out of his evil treasure produces evil, for out of the abundance of the heart his mouth speaks.*
>
> — Luke 6:45 (ESV)

> *For we do not have a high priest who is unable to sympathize with our weaknesses, but one who in every respect has been tempted as we are, yet without sin. Let us then with confidence draw near to the throne of grace, that we may receive mercy and find grace to help in time of need.*
>
> — Hebrews 4:15–16 (ESV)

> *I am speaking in human terms, because of your natural limitations. For just as you once presented your members as slaves to impurity and to lawlessness leading to more lawlessness, so now present your members as slaves to righteousness leading to sanctification. For when you were slaves of sin, you were free in regard to righteousness.*
>
> — Romans 6:19–20 (ESV)

> *What shall we say then? Are we to continue in sin that grace may abound? By no means! How can we who*

died to sin still live in it? Do you not know that all of us who have been baptized into Christ Jesus were baptized into his death? We were buried therefore with him by baptism into death, in order that, just as Christ was raised from the dead by the glory of the Father, we too might walk in newness of life. For if we have been united with him in a death like his, we shall certainly be united with him in a resurrection like his. We know that our old self was crucified with him in order that the body of sin might be brought to nothing, so that we would no longer be enslaved to sin. For one who has died has been set free from sin. Now if we have died with Christ, we believe that we will also live with him. We know that Christ, being raised from the dead, will never die again; death no longer has dominion over him. For the death he died he died to sin, once for all, but the life he lives he lives to God. So you also must consider yourselves dead to sin and alive to God in Christ Jesus. Let not sin therefore reign in your mortal body, to make you obey its passions.

— Romans 6:1–12 (ESV)

Be kind to one another, tenderhearted, forgiving one another, as God in Christ forgave you.

— Ephesians 4:32 (ESV)

But seek first the kingdom of God and his righteousness, and all these things will be added to you.

— Matthew 6:33 (ESV)

When Jesus saw him lying there and knew that he had already been there a long time, he said to him, "Do you want to be healed?"

— John 5:6 (ESV)

Those who regard their own idols forsake their own mercy. But I will sacrifice to You with the voice of thanksgiving. I will pay what I have vowed. Salvation is of the Lord.

— Jonah 2:8–9 (NIV)

Woe to him who strives with him who formed him, a pot among earthen pots! Does the clay say to him who forms it, "What are you making?" or "Your work has no handles"? Woe to him who says to a father, "What are you begetting?" or to a woman, "With what are you in labor?"

— Isaiah 45:9–10 (ESV)

Pride goes before destruction, and a haughty spirit before a fall.

— Proverbs 16:18 (ESV)

We destroy arguments and every lofty opinion raised against the knowledge of God, and take every thought captive to obey Christ, being ready to punish every disobedience, when your obedience is complete.

— 2 Corinthians 10:5–6 (ESV)

And we know that for those who love God all things work together for good, for those who are called according to his purpose. For those whom he foreknew he also predestined to be conformed to the image of his Son, in order that he might be the firstborn among many brothers.

— Romans 8:28–29 (ESV)

Let no corrupting talk come out of your mouths, but only such as is good for building up, as fits the occasion, that it may give grace to those who hear. And do not grieve the Holy Spirit of God, by whom you were sealed for the day of redemption. Let all bitterness and wrath and anger and clamor and slander be put away from you, along with all malice. Be kind to one another, tenderhearted, forgiving one another, as God in Christ forgave you.

— Ephesians 4:29–32 (ESV)

To put off your old self, which belongs to your former manner of life and is corrupt through deceitful desires, and to be renewed in the spirit of your minds, and to put on the new self, created after the likeness of God in true righteousness and holiness.

— Ephesians 4:22–24 (ESV)

So Jesus said to the Jews who had believed him, "If you abide in my word, you are truly my disciples, and you will know the truth, and the truth will set you free."

— John 8:31–32 (ESV)

Sanctify them in the truth; your word is truth.

— John 17:17 (ESV)

Finally, brothers, whatever is true, whatever is honorable, whatever is just, whatever is pure, whatever is lovely, whatever is commendable, if there is any excellence, if there is anything worthy of praise, think about these things. What you have learned and received and heard and seen in me—practice these things, and the God of peace will be with you.

— Philippians 4:8–9 (ESV)

Blessed be the God and Father of our Lord Jesus Christ, the Father of mercies and God of all comfort who comforts us in all our affliction, so that we may be able to comfort those who are in any affliction, with the comfort with which we ourselves are comforted by God. For as we share abundantly in Christ's sufferings, so through Christ we share abundantly in comfort too.

— 2 Corinthians 1:3–5 (ESV)

Therefore, since we have been justified by faith, we have peace with God through our Lord Jesus Christ.

Through him we have also obtained access by faith into this grace in which we stand, and we rejoice in hope of the glory of God. Not only that, but we rejoice in our sufferings, knowing that suffering produces endurance, and endurance produces character, and character produces hope, and hope does not put us to shame, because God's love has been poured into our hearts through the Holy Spirit who has been given to us. For while we were still weak, at the right time Christ died for the ungodly. For one will scarcely die for a righteous person—though perhaps for a good person one would dare even to die—but God shows his love for us in that while we were still sinners, Christ died for us. Since, therefore, we have now been justified by his blood, much more shall we be saved by him from the wrath of God. For if while we were enemies we were reconciled to God by the death of his Son, much more, now that we are reconciled, shall we be saved by his life. More than that, we also rejoice in God through our Lord Jesus Christ, through whom we have now received reconciliation. Therefore, just as sin came into the world through one man, and death through sin, and so death spread to all men because all sinned—for sin indeed was in the world before the law was given, but sin is not counted where there is no law. Yet death reigned from Adam to Moses, even over those whose sinning was not like the transgression of Adam, who was a type of the one who was to come. But the free gift is not like the trespass. For if many died through one man's trespass, much more have the grace of God and the free gift by the grace of that one man Jesus Christ abounded for many. And the free gift is not like the result of that one man's sin. For the judgment following one trespass brought condemnation, but the free gift following many trespasses brought justification. For if, because of one man's trespass, death reigned through that one man, much more will those who receive the abundance of grace and the free gift of righteousness reign in life through the one man Jesus Christ. Therefore, as one trespass led to condemnation for all men, so one act of righteousness leads to justification and life for all men. For as by the one man's disobedience the many were made sinners, so by the one man's obedience the many will be made righteous. Now the law came in to increase the trespass, but where sin increased, grace abounded all the more, so that, as sin reigned in death, grace also might reign through righteousness leading to eternal life through Jesus Christ our Lord.

— Romans 5 (ESV)

Come to me, all who labor and are heavy laden, and I will give you rest. Take my yoke upon you, and learn from me, for I am gentle and lowly in heart, and you will find rest for your souls. For my yoke is easy, and my burden is light.

— Matthew 11:28–30 (ESV)

Or do you not know that your body is a temple of the Holy Spirit within you, whom you have from God?

You are not your own, for you were bought with a price. So, glorify God in your body.

— I Corinthians 6:19–20 (ESV)

CHAPTER 3

Clawing Your Way to the Top (Suicidal Ideology and Depression)

Why are you cast down, O my soul, and why are you in turmoil within me? Hope in God; for I shall again praise him, my salvation.

— Psalm 42:5 (ESV)

I would venture a guess that most people have, at one time or another, had the feeling of depression. Others of you have fallen to the pit at the bottom of depression and see no way out except to end your life. I'm so thankful that God says when life is over and not me. If He is in control of all things, and He is, try as you might, your life will not end until He says it will end.

That's where I was when I let the details of my husband's infidelity nearly drive me crazy. When Dan came back to our family after three weeks away, I thought I could forgive him. I asked God to help me forgive him. But immediately upon seeing him at the airport, I despised even a look at him, knowing he had given away what was ours to another woman.

I decided that I was going to drive us all home, and not give him any control. I was in charge. It was a long, quiet drive, and then I froze. Dan put his foot on the brake and steered us to the side of the highway where I would jump out of the car and heave with great grief, the pain and sorrow so immense that I thought I would die. We traded seats and I leaned my head against the window. I knew at that moment that Jesus was holding me. I was numb and listless, but I heard what was so clear in my mind, *You have one person to forgive. I died to forgive the whole world.*

When Dan had asked me a couple of days before this if he could come home, mind you, an answer to my and others' prayers, I started shopping. I bought all of the things I knew he would need in his brands, like a new toothbrush, toothpaste, shampoo, deodorant, razor, and shaving cream. I knew he had these things, but I did this for two reasons:

1. So that he knew that I know him best and can care for his needs.
2. So that I could throw away everything he brought home after being with someone else.

After he was home, we got rid of those clothes he had taken with him.

The next week was the hardest. Our new pastor at this time was out of town, so we had no one to help us walk through this quagmire of adultery, betrayal, and forgiveness. I became a raving lunatic, acting like I did not have any faith at all. Who was I? This person who had prayed for her husband to come home in repentance could not stand the man she and others at church had prayed for. We searched for a biblical book about adultery and unfortunately read a "Christian" book and listened to a CD with faulty teaching. The author said that whoever the perpetrator of adultery is that the offended should be able to get any detail they want from them when asked. We were so spiritually immature, but I was all for this. I had an insatiable desire to know everything so that I could punish my husband completely. Little did I know that by doing this and by obtaining the details, it would lead me to a deeper, darker depression which almost led me to suicide, if I had had my way.

Our family decided to go to a hotel for a night to get a change of scenery and for the kids to be able to swim. Dan took the kids swimming, and I stayed in the room, drowning in my thoughts and taking the downward spiral into complete darkness. I had let the loss of the idea of an ideal family and husband completely take over my mind. I looked at myself as a statistic and thought that God had failed me. I began taking ibuprofen in large amounts and planning for my suicide. Our oldest daughter (twenty at the time) saw the signs of what I was doing and would resort to slapping the pills out of my hand. At one point, she took the battery out of our car in order to keep me from taking the car and killing myself that way. I'm thankful that she had the foresight to do that, although no child or young adult should have to do this for their parent. It left a mark on our relationship for years that I can never erase but pray that God will continually heal 1,000 times 10,000. He can, and He is.

After we got back home, my husband and our son (seventeen at the time) decided to go to church and then had planned on stopping at the pharmacy for me. I refused to go, and our youngest daughter stayed home with me. I was writing my suicide note even as Dan and our son were leaving the house, unbeknownst to them. I printed it and began my plan. While our youngest daughter (fifteen at the time) was in the shower, I began my very selfish and hopeless plan. I put on my coat, laid out a host of every pill I could find in the house, laid my suicide note on the bed and sat down next to them with my glass of water in hand.

Just at that moment, God intervened by sending my husband and son home early. My sweet daughter knew nothing of my plan and was extremely hurt by this thoughtless act. Providentially, there was no evening service at church that Sunday night, and the pharmacy was already closed. My husband called 911 and an ambulance took my numb and listless body to the hospital, unable to complete my mission. While there, our kids went home to get clothes to stay at a dear teacher's home. They told us the story of walking into the house and that when they went in, something dark shot across the floor and knocked down the chair where I usually sat, splitting the back of the chair.

And thus began the wild and crazy ride of being admitted into the psych ward for three very long days. I was evaluated and, of course, diagnosed with severe depression. I began to see this for what it was and that is oppression of the enemy.

God has a sense of humor which I did not think was funny. The woman who was my roommate shared the same name as the other woman in my husband's life.

This was a very scary three days for me as I was a zombie on new medications, and there were some very dangerously psychotic people on this floor. It took a lot for me to realize that I was acting just like them. I don't remember much about the stay except for that, and the fact that I was labeled as mentally ill. I refused this label and still do. It is not a label I will ever let myself wear as a child of the King. Yes, I was a troubled woman and needed to have help, but the labels placed on people for their life has always been unacceptable. This is not being egotistical, but it leaves no room for being free from that label.

While I was in the hospital, Dan had started a new job, so the youth pastor of our new church and his wife picked me up and dropped me off at home. It was then that I knew that Satan was alive and well in my home. As I walked in the house, the house was burning hot. I checked the thermostat on this winter day, and it was set at sixty-eight degrees. I went through the house and prayed, asking God to forgive me for every part that I had played in allowing Satan to have such a stronghold over me and my family, asking Him to show me how to live a better way and how to forgive.

I was called the next day by the hospital and told that I needed to go to meet with a psychiatrist to get my medications. I went to this appointment and was given enough sleeping pills and antidepressants in a personal belongings bag to end my life. I thought this very odd. I did, however, take these pills faithfully in hopes of coming out of the dark.

After being home for another week, Dan and my dad thought it would be good for us to get a fresh start and to come to Tennessee where he and my mom lived. They traveled a lot for mission trips and would be gone most of the time, so the house would be ours for the most part.

I told my husband that I was not going anywhere with him unless there was a biblical counselor in the area. So, we got on the website for the organization I was familiar with to search for a biblical counselor (NANC previously, now ACBC: www.biblicalcounseling.com). God had placed a man (this man has now been our pastor for over seventeen years) just five minutes away from my parents' home, and there was no doubt in my mind that we should make this move. I sent him an email telling him our story and he wrote back telling me that he was very concerned and gave me Romans 15:4 to hold onto until we arrived in Tennessee, and he could meet with us.

We were blessed with church family at our new church who intervened in a big way. I was in such a numb and depressed state that I could not do anything by this time, so they helped Dan and the kids to pack up our entire house for our trip to Tennessee. Surprisingly I drove part of the way to Tennessee while our son drove a fair share; my dear son who had spent days visiting the cemetery when his dad was away from us. He was aware of what Dan was going to do in leaving us before Dan told the rest of us and thus had a lot of weight to bear with what he fittingly saw as a death in our family. Each one of our kids shared a very heavy weight during this time and for a long time until they saw true reconciliation in my and Dan's marriage.

A couple of days after our arrival to my parents' home, my dad asked if I would like to go with him a couple of hours away while he took care of business and that he would get me my own hotel room and I could just get a break from everything. I hugged my husband goodbye and whispered to him that I was never coming back.

But God! That evening when Dad and I were having dinner, I told him that I did not want to go back to Dan. He didn't expect this as part of his moving plan and told me that we would talk about it in the morning, that I should get some rest and see how I felt the next day.

The next morning when I awoke from another almost sleepless night, I sat in the chair of my room, threw my Bible open rather abruptly, and told God that He either spoke to me that day or I was done with Him. This is not my recommendation as I meant no disrespect to God at that moment, but He knew me and met me there in my desperation. I looked down at my Bible and it was open to Jonah 2, and I read it out loud and started crying.

I did go back home to my husband that day and shared with him how God had so clearly met me in His Word. I challenge you to look at that passage of Scripture for yourself and to read it out loud. In fact, I challenge you to read your Bible out loud at any time. From that moment on, I knew that I had a Savior I could trust to care for me in this crisis and beyond.

I wish I could say that it was easy to live and walk away from the pain of betrayal. It was the hardest thing I had ever done in choosing to stay with my husband. He was changing and becoming the person God had meant for him to be; we were receiving counseling for our marriage, and I was stuck. The suicidal thoughts returned with full force. I even began for a short time to cut myself with a nail file. The brain chooses the pain, and any pain was better than the pain of betrayal and hating myself.

I decided that I could not take these sleeping pills and antidepressants anymore, and not because anyone recommended me to stop. I had previously had to wean myself off psychotropics after the molestation of our child years earlier, knowing that the suicidal thoughts would only get worse the longer I stayed on them. In a midnight hour, my husband called our pastor when I was talking about killing myself. Our pastor asked for me to get my Bible. I opened Mom and Dad's large family Bible that was on the table and began to read the verses that he would point me to. God's truths broke through my hard heart, and it was the beginning of learning how to find my answers in Scripture to help me in my walk of faith, out of the woods and into His freedom. That freedom was five years in the making to be able to not be triggered by everything that brought back the details of my husband's adultery. We went through another earth-shattering (would be family-shattering) time after that which led to Dan's salvation, of which I am most thankful. We were blessed to have our pastor to walk through every part of this that we would let him into, and he and his wife were very instrumental in our staying together.

Below is my husband's wonderful testimony, one of true repentance that he has continually walked out ever since. He is very supportive of me writing this book and of sharing what God has redeemed.

Dan's Testimony to the Grace of God

> Grace: *"The unmerited and abundant gift of God's love for man."*

In November 2006, a series of events began that would forever change my life and the lives of my family. The direction we were going at that time appeared to be appropriate, noble, and ordained by God. As God has taught me since then, I know that it was His divine appointment to take us from where we were and bring us through those painful, critical moments in the months to follow.

No matter how noble I believed my intentions were, my life was like the one described in Matthew 15:8; I honored the Lord with my lips, but my heart was far away from Him. There was sin in my life that had not been confessed and those sins were "finding me out." My response to this exposure of sin resulted in running … running from God, running from facing the truth of an unregenerate heart, and running from a precious, devastated family.

How thankful I am for the relentless pursuit of God in His love and saving grace. In spite of the delusional life I was involved in, God brought me back home to face His truth and *begin* the reconciliation process with Him, my wife, and children. I emphasize the word "begin" because it has been a most difficult and long process.

Yet as difficult as it has been God, has been faithful to show His ability to restore and make beautiful those things which were so broken and seemingly beyond repair—they were beyond the repair of human intervention alone.

> *In him we have redemption through his blood, the forgiveness of our trespasses, according to the riches of his grace*
>
> — Ephesians 1:7 (ESV)

For by grace you have been saved through faith, and that not of yourselves; it is the gift of God, not of works, lest anyone should boast.

— Ephesians 2:8–9 (NKJV)

How wonderful God in His grace used my broken, hurting wife to speak the truth to my lost condition in December of 2007. I am so thankful she was there with me when my heart truly and completely became God's!

For it is God who works in you, both to will and to work for his good pleasure.

— Philippians 2:13 (ESV)

I will never get over how God established the way before us by putting Pastor Mark Mann and the believers of Grace Bible Fellowship into our lives. He ordained these brothers and sisters to help bring healing, accountability, and love. I pray now as God allows my life to continue that it will reflect the words found in Acts 20:24 (NASB):

> "But I do not consider my life of any account as dear to myself, so that I may finish my course and the ministry which I received from the Lord Jesus, to testify solemnly of the gospel of God's grace."

CHAPTER 4

Mistrust of a Lifetime

Trust in the Lord with all your heart, and do not lean on your own understanding.
In all your ways acknowledge him, and he will make straight your paths.

— Proverbs 3:5–6 (ESV)

My life as a caregiver was brought on by those who would take away care.

I played the role of a caretaker as a child and that continued until my parents died in 2023. I'm not sure why they call it caretaking, as in its right and proper perspective, it should be caregiving. But as a child and until I was married, the care was being taken away from me by the pure reason that I had to be everything for my dad and my mom, constantly giving what I did not have to give and that being pretending happiness for them; that also being feelings of guilt for everyone that had to cross paths with my dysfunctional biological family.

As faulty as this thinking was, I felt that my caregiving and responsibility in my family began at conception. My parents got pregnant with me in November of 1963, got married in January of 1964, and gave birth to me in July of 1964. When they became pregnant with me, my mom already had three sons that I would later learn were my half-brothers and Dad already had a failed marriage and a daughter. I will always call them my brothers and sister, though, as that is what they are, and always will be to me, even though I was not raised with this sister but with a sister who would be born to my parents eleven and a half months after my birth.

As a young child and teen, I wished so badly that they had never gotten pregnant with me so that they would not be together, as when they were, my dad was very angry. He was very angry no matter who he was with. The fact is that when me and my siblings were little, when he was home, we were afraid. There are so many painful memories that I never had the courage to share with him, nor to confront him with while he was alive. I am only able to write freely now since he passed away on February 23, 2023. I knew that I was his little favorite, and everyone in the family knew it. I hated being a favorite!

My mom was so very sad on so many days when he was home. The relief and joy that she exhibited to us kids when my dad was working late or was out of town for work was like night and day to me, and perhaps to all of us. We had a seasonal dad when we were pre-teens and teens, as Dad worked as a commercial roofer in the cold north. He eventually owned his own commercial roofing/insulation company that every kid in our family at one time or another worked in. It was expected and we all knew it, whether in the office or in the field. Once any of us began to work in the family business, it had to become our whole world in order to be accepted by and to please our dad.

One of my earlier memories of my father was when my dad had my oldest brother shoot our dogs. I was given a dog named Rex for my birthday. We also had a dog named Rowdy when I was a little girl living in Ohio on our beautiful farm before the age of nine. One day, and I believe it was a Saturday or a Sunday because Dad was home, a nearby farmer came knocking on the door of our Ohio farmhouse. Or maybe a neighbor called and told us about it … a child's mind can play tricks on them, and they usually remember the truth, but it gets mixed up in their head. There is something that is not mixed up at all. The neighbor's sheep had gotten stuck in the mud, and the neighbor said that our dogs were trying to kill the sheep. As an adult, I now hear how absurd that would be for our friendly farm dogs to turn like that and kill sheep.

The result of that knock on our door, or that phone call received, was that my dad gave my fourteen or fifteen-year-old brother a rifle and told him to go and shoot the dogs because we could not have our dogs bothering the neighbors' sheep. He said this in the hearing of all of us little ones. And then the curtains were closed in the dining room and living room while Steve went to "take care of this." My dog Rex and our dog Rowdy were both shot that day.

I often think of what a heavy burden this had to be on my oldest brother to be commanded to be a part of this horrific task. I vowed to never love another animal ever again that day for fear that if I did, my dad would kill it.

That is my memory of the whole event. I also know now that I had this "other" dad at that time that was just beginning to be discipled in his faith. This is not me excusing his behavior nor this event, nor the damage it did to my family.

The problem is that I saw this kind of harsh behavior for most of his life. I am not God, and I truly trust that when He saves a soul, He saves completely, so I have begun to trust that God had to deal with Dad's heart needing to surrender his way for a lifetime. Dad struggled as Paul of the Bible did in doing the things he did not want to do and not doing the things that he wanted to do. Dad had a very painful past that he never dealt with and some of that I found out after his death.

No amount of ball games in the front yard, nor rides in the back of his pickup truck, nor pails of homemade ice cream would ever replace that little girl's dog, nor her broken heart. I am missing complete memory of the second and third grade of my life, and perhaps that is part of it.

During the summer of 1973, after my third grade year, without any notice to us as kids, or at least to me, or perhaps I was so distraught that I could not remember, our family packed up and moved away from that beloved farmhouse which me and my siblings had enjoyed so much. I remember thinking that we would be back and that we were just going on vacation. I did not know what a moving truck was, and I don't remember packing anything up, nor having an explanation—nothing at all.

Perhaps this older woman needs to part with that house, as also in that house was where I was first sexually molested by others and in that barn, the same. I think there is a big secret hiding in my very dark soul of what happened in the potato shed at that house. Why would I associate so many good memories with such a place? Maybe it's because I was a compliant little kid that thought I was doing the right thing with pleasing people and keeping secrets for them. Maybe it is because I was trusting as a child. Maybe it's because it's where we learned to have fun even when Dad came home. He would join the family in ball games in the front yard, play washers with us, get us involved in gardening, and take us to church every Sunday morning and night and any time the church doors were open.

When I was about nine or ten years old, after leaving my beloved farm, my parents brought us all into the kitchen and told us they had something that they wanted to tell us. They told us that my brothers were not my and my sister's full blood brothers and that mom had all three of them before she married my dad. Perhaps they had to tell us that because one day it would all come out anyway. But the world changed that day for me.

I already knew that my dad had a daughter, my older sister, from a previous marriage, and unfortunately, another brother of mine who did not live from that marriage. All I ever heard about was how bad that marriage was, if I heard anything at all. He thought it strange that his daughter did not want to spend time with him. I thought it was just about right. Why should she when he did not have her in his life really? When she visited us once or twice, my mom despised her, this mom who in her former unregenerate life had had many men in her life prior to marrying my dad. She could not bear the thought of Dad having been with my sister's mother as his wife.

It's interesting; there is so much that I don't know about their past lives that they would not talk about, but I would hear about from others. It's all mixed up in my mind even at my current age.

What I do remember is that I started at such a young age to want to hurt myself. When I was around eight, back at the farmhouse, I purposefully stepped on a bumblebee when my aunt and uncle came to visit, just to get attention. At the age of nine, after having moved to Wisconsin, I held my breath for attention when my brother had friends over until I fainted and hit my head on the coffee table. As I regained consciousness, I woke up with a bleeding cut on my eyebrow and no one paying me any attention.

Fast-forward to a month or two after my parents told our family about my brothers not being full blood to us. I certainly became fresh meat to the fleshly desires of many friends of my brothers, and I didn't dare tell anyone about this. I feared the wrath of my dad more than I feared the misuse of my body. I was not being protected as a sister should be. A couple of days after that revealing conversation, I went outside where there was a piece of wood with nails pointing out of it. I stomped down as hard as I could on that nail so that it went through my tennis shoe and into my foot. I screamed and mom came running out and took me to the doctor for a look and a tetanus shot. The misuse/abuse of my body happened from the time I was about five or six until about eleven years old when my mother asked me if someone had been touching me in private places. I told her yes, and she became more vigilant of watching out for me, but it was never enough, as I sought ways to get attention from boys in manipulative ways.

About a year or two after this conversation about my brothers, as I was doing a little math on my parent's wedding anniversary, I started to realize that the amount of the years of their wedding anniversary was the same amount of the years that I was old, just seven months later after their wedding anniversary. I then figured out that year, when I was about thirteen or fourteen, that they *had to get married* because of me. I screamed. I hollered. I cried for all the pain that I had caused. They poo-pooed even the mention of it, and thought I was being too emotional. I heard that my whole life about everything as I felt everything very deeply. And that was the end of that conversation, because Dad said so. Emotions that were real versus real physical pain were never accepted.

It was, however, not the end of the root of bitterness that had already begun to take up residency in my heart toward both of my parents for making me responsible for all their sins and for all the anger that would show up in our family, unless we just made Dad happy. Better not anyone disturb any of Dad's happiness, or his world, his kingdom or there was his wrath to pay. It reared its ugly head on so many occasions over the years that I could not even, nor do I want to, mention them all. Dad would teach Sunday school (and the church better let him). But we kept going to church, putting on a happy face to not embarrass or make Dad mad. Sunday afternoons were the worst. Dad was tired. Dad needed to rest; don't wake him up. *Shhhhh*, let's go for a walk; let's go fishing; let's do anything away from home so Dad could sleep.

That is, until one day that sleep got disturbed. My sister and I had gone fishing at a pond a mile or two away, and it wasn't long after that we saw Sonny and Todd and Mom walking toward us. I think my sister and I were about ten and nine years old at this time. We asked them what they were doing, and my brothers spilled the story, and my mom excused it all. One of the boys had made a sound and awakened my dad, and

I'm glad I was not there. I do not know what happened, but it was bad, and they were all shaken by the time they got to the pond. We were then all afraid to go home. Of course, when we got home, Dad had an excuse.

On another occasion, my eleven-year-old brother, Todd, complained about what we were eating for dinner. Or maybe my dad complained about the meal. It was hash made from Sunday's wonderful roast beef meal. Anyway, whether my brother complained about the meal or perhaps said something to my dad about his response to my mom about the meal, the next thing we all knew is that my dad jerked my brother up and threw him down the three to four steps that led to the family room of our house. I despised leftovers after that, and mom was sure to never make leftovers again. We no longer had mixed meals or casseroles because Dad did not like them.

One night during that same time frame as the fishing incident and the hash incident, my oldest brother was picked up driving with an open container of alcohol in the car. My sister's and my bedroom was off the kitchen. I woke up to my oldest brother, Steve, crying and my dad screaming sarcastically at him, telling him to "Drink it! You want to drink and drive; you will drink every bit of it!" There was a six or twelve pack of beer on the table that my brother was made to drink all of. Oh, my poor Steve. But what could I do? I was bustled back to bed by my crying mother to "go to sleep." I curled up into a ball and cried.

After my dad started his own business, his life became even more stressful, and so did ours. When I was a teenager, one time I ran up to him and sat on his lap. Dad was very uncomfortable and told me that I was too old to be sitting on his lap. Really? This girl needed her daddy's loving and safe touch and to be shown how God loves us so unconditionally and does not shame us. So, I sought for love from every boy and man that came along. So he had a terrible childhood and first marriage. Was that my fault? Was that my mom's fault? Why did he take his terrible life out on us? Why, even at his old and retired age that he was when I started to write this chapter, was he so angry and such a grudge holder? Why was enough never enough? Why were there so many expectations placed on me, and why have I felt so much guilt? From the time I was a teenager, I can remember feeling like my dad loved me more than he loved my mom. Also, my mom and I did not really get along for a very long time, and mainly only began to be able to show our love for each other when I was in my mid-forties. Sadly, that was too late as Mom was soon to be diagnosed with early onset dementia.

As a teen, when Dad was out of town for work, my mom was so very mistrusting of what he was doing while he was out of town that she used to cry and then she would tell me about what some women had done in flirting with him, and how she knew that Dad was attracted to them and that she did not find herself to be pretty anymore. I began to despise him for making my mom feel this way, at least in my mind, but never spoke of it. I began to despise the women who would flirt with my dad, as told to me by my mom. Never would I tell her that I was now this type of girl. I couldn't. I knew she bore so much shame in her own life that even as a young teen, I knew I couldn't. I used to demand that my mom needed to divorce Dad for the things that I was hearing, and I felt she was weak to put up with the anger that she and we all endured.

My dad was no different. He would take me out and confide in me that Mom just had a lot on her and was jealous, and that he was so unhappy, and he just needed for me to be better with Mom (as if it was all my fault) and that he knew I could. He expected me to be a good girl so Mom and I could get along.

And as I grew older and had my own children, my thoughts turned to, *Why on earth would a woman or a man ever tell their children about these things? Why would a parent ever confide in their children as if they were an adult that could help them?* Oh, what pain and hate and distrust that cultivated in my own heart and mind. I mistrusted, and at times still struggle with mistrusting every man in the world and think of them all as fornicators and adulterers, or on their way there. I mistrusted, and at times still do, every woman in the world and think of them as husband-stealers who will one day win against the weak man, and have her way with them, or that the weak man will overpower the woman to have his way with her and then be done with her. This is faulty thinking and one in which I grew up with and saw come to fruition in my own marriage, and one which I have humbly reconciled with Jesus Christ, so that I am forgiving and showing acts worthy of repentance. I am not, however, perfect and do war with my flesh and ungodly thinking in this area, and so I pray with the rest of you that our hearts would be completely His and our minds constantly renewed to steel ourselves against the very real wiles of Satan in this area.

We were always told that what happens at our house is our business, and we are not to talk to anyone about our family. I learned how to lie and deceive to not incur the wrath of my dad so he would think that I was a good girl. My siblings caught on to that and used me to be the one who gave believable excuses to our folks when we were late arriving home or needed to explain what happened with anything that may have gone wrong. I became a great liar. It didn't matter to me at all because I felt that all of life was a lie … my happiness, my folks' marriage, church people, and I'm sure so much more. I learned how to manipulate and was good at it. I sadly gave away my virginity when I was thirteen years old, and my brother heard about it and laughed. I cried and would find every opportunity until I met my husband to keep using guys and letting them use me. As I aged out of my parents' house by way of marriage, I hated myself for who I was and what I had allowed myself to become with other boys. I not only did not know who I was, but I certainly did not ever believe anything my husband told me. I did not believe what anyone told me. I trusted no one because I could not trust myself.

    For as long as I can remember, I recall my dad controlling everything and bossing everyone around who didn't do things his way, whether that was people on a job, people in our schools or in our church, innocent people who had nothing to do with him but said something that didn't sit well in his kingdom. He was seventy-nine years old at the beginning of my writing this chapter (he passed at eighty in 2023), and he may not have been outwardly vocal toward people in person like he used to be, but he was not content until he was talking about someone or putting someone down and still screamed at people on the phone, in the car while driving, and in public places. I hated to go anywhere with him! It was so embarrassing to walk in every restaurant and walk out because something was wrong with the food or we did not get seated quickly enough.

Dad was very impatient with my Alzheimer's-ridden mom. The act that he shined on in front of me and my husband and others, using a baby voice in showing his love to my mom, had to be one big act. Why would this angry man be okay now that she poops her pants, pees on the floor and the bed, and costs him so much money in her care? Is that caregiving or caretaking? I'm confused as from a very young age that has become a very mixed-up mess in my head. Why would he never stop taking and taking and expecting so much from me in her care when I had a family of my own? Why on earth did we ever move to any areas near where my parents lived?

Yes, God had His plans for a beginning to His healing of my heart with our move to Tennessee in 2007. Oh man, I thought I was learning to love and trust and to forgive all the people in the world—ha! Not funny because I had grown so accustomed to acquiescing to my dad's demands that I began once again to fortify my kingdom with an attitude of bitterness now directed toward my dad. I began to look at him as my enemy.

As you may be aware of by now, and I want to be very clear when I say that *he's not the enemy, she's not the enemy, and neither is HE*, that we all have an enemy, and he is real, and his name is Satan. It does us no good to just state that others are not our enemies but to clarify who the enemy of our soul is. Satan has made it his mission, ever since his beguiling efforts in the garden of Eden, to twist God's Words and to make them fit man's and woman's desires instead of reclaiming our image that was lost on that God-ordained day in the garden. We are told in John 10:10 (ESV) that "the thief comes only to steal and kill and destroy. I came that they may have life and have it abundantly."

God has our best and His glory in mind in every circumstance or situation. Satan's motive is to destroy the believer and to negate the glory of God and to make the child of God useless for any of God's kingdom purposes. "Be sober-minded; be watchful. Your adversary the devil prowls around like a roaring lion, seeking someone to devour" (1 Peter 5:8, ESV).

May that someone not be you, dear child of God. Put on your armor, the armor of the Word of God and truth and stand firm against the onslaught of Satan. Do not hear me say that you are to rebuke the devil. Even Jesus only used God's Word to stand against the devil. We have no power in this fight except through immersing ourselves in God's Word so that we may recount what we have learned when the enemy would seek to slaughter us in our thoughts and in our actions.

CHAPTER 5

Messing with My Kingdom

For it is God who works in you, both to will and to work for his good pleasure.

— Philippians 2:13 (ESV)

God started to mess with this kingdom of mine which I had built just like my father, and I'm so glad that He did. I have needed every rebuke that He has brought my way. But this, Lord?

In 2020, out of the blue, I became stuck in a frozen state after hearing a shrill shriek in my right ear and could not speak or move for hours. The ambulance came and my husband and they thought I had just had a stroke. This was not the case, and these issues have come under control with medical care now in 2024. The symptoms significantly reduced a year after the death of both of my parents last year within twenty-five days of each other.

This present sickness made no sense to me. Just when there began to be much peace in our home, and we were serving God freely without the bondage of past sins by us and against us, I was stricken with this paralyzing of my mind and body for over three years about three to five times per week, thus being incapacitated. What was it that I was to learn? I prayed for godly wisdom and joy. I wanted to learn it and not to just make life easier (although that would have been nice) but to truly walk in faithfulness toward God because of my love for Him and because of His great love for me.

> *I must say, Lord, that as much as I am convinced that Your Word has, like You say, "all things that pertain to life and godliness" (2 Peter 1:3, ESV), that I got very tired of the Christian-ese, the throwing out of Scripture to my life as if people were hoping that it would stick on me such as in Job's counselors. I am thankful for You and for Your Word, and for how it has saved my life, and how it is continually changing my heart, and yet cliches for me are deceitful coping mechanisms that Christians use on each other when they don't know how to listen first, don't know what to say, when they don't know how to comfort with the comfort with which they have been comforted, and don't know how to talk someone through God's providence.*

Sometimes it is just a listening ear and a prayer that helps the most. I speak that to my own chagrin as well. Shoot, sometimes I don't even know how to comfort myself nor anyone else with the comfort with which I have been comforted. I'm being real, people. The enemy of this world, Satan, seeks to steal, kill, and destroy. I have sought the Lord consistently to not allow me to be a victim of this thievery. There is a real lack of teaching on God's providential sovereignty in the church. There is a real lack of biblical soul care being taught to the church. There is a real lack of the church teaching against sinful responses to the circumstances that God has allowed (not caused) in our lives.

I am weak from so much happening in my life since 2007 when my husband left me for another woman for three agonizing weeks, and having to move to another state, give up on my dreams of serving on a foreign mission field, having so much suffering since then, our daughter coming home from college pregnant (which has led to the joy of our wonderful grandson), and since our daughter had supraventricular tachycardia in 2010 followed by my dad having a heart attack in 2010, Mom being diagnosed with dementia in 2011, my husband finally getting back to a job that could meet our needs, and the need for me to work so hard to help make ends meet even when I was so sick, of the fact that at a few months away from being thirty-five years old, our daughter received the dreaded diagnosis of breast cancer, which is thankfully now in remission. I am weary from our having helped to start a church in 2007 with a small group of believers and the many friendships we have lost along the way as people have consistently left the church. God knows what I can handle, and I have strived to have faith and to trust Him knowing that His ways are best, and I have learned so much about Him through all of this. Dear one, I understand your pain, although it is different than mine, and most likely in intensity, but I beg of you to let Jesus Christ help you to carry these heavy burdens.

Everything that I thought I may have learned about biblical counseling, where the Bible is sufficient for every one of my needs, was brought into question as I was referred for cognitive behavioral therapy to deal with non-epileptic seizures brought on by what they are calling post-traumatic stress disorder, on top of ongoing Meniere's disease and at times the continued die-off of Lyme's disease. In my research, there is nothing that can be done for non-epileptic seizures except to medicate gently and to seek help to deal with the things that I have experienced in my life through cognitive behavioral therapy. I have already dealt specifically at the cross of Christ with these issues of the past, and so to seek cognitive behavioral therapy to stop having seizures was not what I desired to do. It took over 144 hours of EEGs and five neurologists all saying the same thing for me to be accepting of this diagnosis.

How I can sit and talk until I'm blue in the face with the world's counselors, and how that will help is beyond me as I have sought biblical counseling for years. But I have done so with faith, and God has helped me to come out of the paralyzing episodes and seizures. I am grateful for my therapist and her gentle way of guiding me to talk. I am so grateful to have my concentration level being restored, and my mental abilities to come back.

Who knows what the rest of the story will be? I will cling to my Savior and His Word as I know I can trust Him and He will not let me go. He is faithful and always will be. Yes, indeed, I do feel that root of darkness at times starting to creep its ugly tentacles into my heart and mind again but know that I am powerless without the Word of God and prayer to fight this and no longer have strength to do so. It is God's strength that heals my weaknesses and His control that I cling to. This world is not just about me, and I am so keenly aware of that. I know that there is a God that loves me and has a plan for me that I do not know of and that He is the one in control of all things and that His mysteries are without my understanding and without my permission.

I just wanted to have a break from my memories of anger, heartache, and sorrow, from people molesting kids, from husbands leaving their wife and children, from Lyme's disease, from mold toxicity, from heavy metal poisoning, from neurological soup, from Alzheimer's, from death, from expectations and guilt, and the erroneous feeling that I would NEVER be enough for anything, anyone, nor for any situation. I wanted to feel like I could concentrate on my job that I was being paid to do. I wanted to feel again, more than I felt such pain in my past. Part of this is the pain of grief and relief of my parents' passing, which I will write about in another chapter.

As a start to heal from what they say is conversion disorder caused from PTSD and abuse, I wrote a letter to my dad. When he was seventy-eight years old with a new diagnosis of pulmonary fibrosis, I could not get a break from his expectations of my total care for him and Mom. That is my next chapter. It hurts me to read it and yet I had a lifetime of stored up sorrow and needed for him to hear how his expectations had affected me in my sickened state and perhaps even contributed to it.

CHAPTER 6

A Letter to My Dad (Unrealistic Imposed Expectations)

> *As* a father shows compassion to his children, *so the LORD shows compassion to those who fear him. For he knows our frame; he remembers that we are dust.*
>
> — Psalm 103:13–14 (ESV)

It was with a great deal of anguish and yet love for this father of mine who called himself a believer and follower of Christ that I wrote this letter. I wish I could say that it made a positive impact in our relationship but just the opposite was true. Since I was no longer acquiescing to his every demand, it made Dad even angrier and brought him into an apathetic mode with me. I did, however, care for him and for Mom but no longer according to his demands and only when I felt well enough to do so in short amounts of time. I did it as being honoring to my father and no longer because I had to.

> Dad,
> I was actually in shock today after reading your texts to me this morning and even more grieved that you have no sympathy as my dad for my life and my

health, job situation, and the fact that I had a full day of helping Bethany with her kids while she thought Zoe may have aspirated something into her lungs.

Dad, the way you conduct yourself in family relationships is abusive. You have established "laws" that, if they are not complied with, incur your wrath. You treat people in ways that seek to manipulate them into obeying your commands. Your "punishments" include harsh texts designed to inflict guilt for disobeying, severing the relationship altogether, or threatening to move away.

You are my father, and I love you. Yet, you have chosen to define love in your own way according to what you can gain from the relationship, which is selfish and self-serving. You are torn up and miserable because you are not submitting to the Lord in the circumstances of your life, and you are very discontent at what He has allowed to happen to you and Mom. That's not my responsibility but yours. You've done this to yourself. You have made it impossible for me to continue a relationship with you by your selfish way of acting when you refuse to think of anyone but yourself.

Look at what continually happens in this "relationship." Whenever you do not hear from me, you text me and tell me that you are moving or that you are traveling overseas or sit in my living room and tell me you are putting Mom in a nursing home so you can travel overseas or other things intended to make me feel bad. That's manipulation. It grieves me that you don't even see this as a pattern of your life and so the cycle repeats itself.

You've made it impossible for me to continue a father/daughter relationship with you. This pattern that has defined our relationship through the years is sinful and dishonoring to God. And now it has become detrimental to my physical health. The unhealthy, ungodly pattern that you've established, and I've allowed, has never been dealt with biblically through genuine conviction, confession, and true repentance. Well, Dad, as much as I've hoped and prayed and waited for genuine repentance, it has not happened.

So, I'm confessing my failure to hold you accountable for the sinful way you've treated us family members. I've allowed you to strike fear of man in me, and I've allowed you to manipulate me through threats and false guilt. I've failed to love you as my father by fearing you more than God and by capitulating to your demands, allowing the cycle to continue through the years. Those are my sins before God. I confess them to you, seeking both God's forgiveness and yours. Sadly, my act of repentance from these things means I must now turn away from this relationship. To allow it to continue in its present state would only compound the sin on both of our parts.

I grieve for you as I have proven my love over and over by acts of service, and yet you do not see it. These are the consequences of your life as you have run roughshod over many people over the years and have talked about them behind their back. I have spoken to *you about that oftentimes, and sometimes have been silent, and there is always an excuse, and never do I hear anything about it being a disgrace to the Lord. I always suspected that one day it would be my turn to receive the wrath that has been inflicted on others, and now I am yet again the recipient of this hatred. You have shipwrecked so many of your relationships, and only when someone is subservient to your requests and does things on your terms is there any hope of any kind of a relationship with you. That is not a loving relationship; it's an ungodly, unhealthy, legalistic arrangement.*

For the sake of my health and my spiritual health, I am choosing to not be submissive to this behavior anymore. I am not okay with just making nice. I am praying for true conviction. Biblically, it is past time as this has become a life-degenerating cycle. I am done with you playing with my emotions in order to save money instead of you getting the physical caregiving that you and Mom both need. That is a terrible thing to do to your daughter, and I am convinced that God cannot be pleased with that. We are both suffering the consequences of this because we have not handled problems God's way.

I have become an abused codependent in this relationship and will not do so anymore. I refuse to be complicit with not speaking the truth in love, failing to walk out this repentance on my part. Please forgive me for not dealing with this biblically by repenting of my fear of man and accepting the false guilt you inflict on me. I write this with all sincerity and love for God and you. I am telling you as your sister in Christ that you need to repent.

You have done permanent harm to others, including me. Today, I am grieved that you leave me no choice but to sever our relationship. For the sake of my marriage and my family (your grandchildren and great grandchildren) and my health and healing. It grieves me to speak this truth, and yet I must because that is what love does. I believe it is what Christ would have me do. I am praying for you.

Love, Marcia

Do you have someone in your life that you need to be honest with? Perhaps it is a controlling or angry parent or spouse that knows the Lord and needs to know that the way they are treating you is not okay or that it is abusive. Some of you may think that it is too late or that it has gone on so long that the offending person will never change. Have you bathed this person in prayer and sought God as to how you should address this person?

Are you being truthful with this person? The reason is never to make yourself feel better to have "gotten it out finally." The reason is a God-honoring desire to confront your sister or brother in Christ. If your motive is to get them to change for you, this change will never last.

Their response to your words in written or verbal form is not your responsibility. Your heart must be pure in this, seeking Christ to give you the words that will honor Him as you go.

You may need the help of a pastor/counselor to help you with the words, and that is okay. At the end of the day, though, whatever you have to say to the offender is to be godly.

CHAPTER 7

Relationships Don't Always Get Healed on Earth (Death)

Light dawns in the darkness for the upright; he is gracious, merciful, and righteous.

— Psalm 112:4 (ESV)

Dad received the diagnosis of pulmonary fibrosis on October 31, 2019, while coming out of anesthesia after back surgery. I was there as I always was for every hospitalization of him and of Mom. I felt it was my duty, and that was the problem. It was my duty out of expectations put on me from the time I was a young girl to make everyone happy. I was their advocate, and I do not regret that at all. After Dad was officially confirmed in this diagnosis, in a couple of weeks by a pulmonologist, we were told that patients with this diagnosis only have two to five years to live. Dad felt that he had already used one of those years as he told me he had been struggling to breathe for a while.

I died a little more inside as I felt mercy for his condition but also knew that he was continuing to travel overseas for mission trips and that I would be called on to help even more.

Thankfully, I have a husband who knows my limits and was my gauge for when I could do something to help Mom and Dad and when it was beyond my capability. My husband, as well as my brother who lives nearby, shouldered a large share of this load as well. My brother and I had already been caring for Mom in order that Dad could have less lifting and care for her with her Alzheimer's.

I began scheduling caregiving for Mom in their home in early 2018. Dad was totally in control as it was "his home," and he made sure to let every caregiver and me know this. We had many caregivers that quit after a day or two of my training them. In most cases, Dad would fire them, and I would find another one. The caregiver we had in early 2019 was truly great with Mom but got an offer of a better position and took it. With that, she brought a totally untrained young woman into their home with the promise of training her. She trained her once, unfortunately. Dad was not happy but looked at her as someone that God had brought into their home that he might evangelize her. And so, he did, and not without his constant complaining to her at the same time. I used to feel sorry for her for the misrepresentation of the gospel that this was presenting.

She was inexperienced as a caregiver and Dad knew it and so did I. I struggled to find another caregiver during the pandemic but couldn't find those willing to go into people's homes, so she had to stay, and I trained her as best as I could in between my days of seizing. I was against her care from the beginning, but Dad would only pay for a low-priced caregiver for mom and that is what we were stuck with for three very long years.

After I began to have my health struggles in March of 2020, Mom and Dad traveled to the Philippines. Mom in her demented state and Dad with his breathing issues. He was not yet on oxygen. It was always a relief when they would travel as I was not called on for everything. I told my husband that if they were still traveling that I did not feel any responsibility to be their caregivers.

Upon their return, and while I was in the throes of paralyzing neurological episodes, I was continually called on to order supplies for Mom, help with meals, and go to their home two blocks away to help with something. If I was not called on, my husband was. This was very wearing on us as we struggled for my health to get better, had a tornado hit our house in March of 2020, and needed to get our home back in order. After two months of being out of our house at a hotel with renovations being done on our home, and my constant seizures, Mom and Dad's conditions were deteriorating. I knew I was the best caregiver for them, but I could no longer do this. We also had five grandchildren and three adult kids of our own. Any times that I felt well enough to do so, we would spend time with them or attempt for me to go to church or visit with our church family.

Dad always had an expectation that I needed to plan everything for them or rise to the occasion of having someone else to do so from his church. We did not attend the same church, so this was a big ask as I was afraid of the questions of why I would not be doing these things I was asking of them. Dad was a proud man and did not want to ask for himself. It took a lot for me to ask him to call his church and seek those needs to be met by them on his own. He was already mad because he said no one visited him and Mom. When he asked, they were happy to help, and did, even in their own painful state as one suffering lady would often come to bring joy and assistance to Mom.

My brain was a neurological soup, and I only had bandwidth to concentrate on my real estate job when I could but needed to do so to help us make ends meet. Thankfully, God provided during these times in ways I can't even begin to explain.

At the end of 2022, Mom was hospitalized with a recurrent drug-resistant UTI over Thanksgiving. On Thanksgiving Day of 2022, I had a new caregiver who was trained in caregiving and nursing to start to care for Mom at the hospital. This caregiver was such a godsend. She loved and protected Mom immensely and at times stepped in to train the other caregiver to do her job better so that Mom would be safe when she was not there. This caregiver, Mary, has become one of my dearest friends, even beyond the death of my parents.

Not too long after Mom was discharged from the hospital and in a rehabilitation center, I had to take Dad to a scheduled pulmonology appointment. The pulmonologist sent him directly across the road by ambulance as his oxygen was down to seventy. He told us that Dad may only have two weeks to live, and most likely not more than that. He suggested that while Dad was hospitalized that we have hospice come to the hospital. So, we did.

Dad's breathing was somewhat regulated, or at least enough to ask the right questions of the hospice representative while they visited in his hospital room. Mom had been in the hospital and rehabilitation for three weeks by this time with no improvement. So, we made the decision together that hospice would come to my parent's house for both of my parents.

Hospice came into their home on January 10 of 2023. My siblings and Dad's brothers and others from out of state came in to visit as a goodbye to Mom and Dad, and we were able to have refreshing times with my dad that in our whole lifetime most of our family never had. He did not have to take any hospice medications until the end of January as the breathing became so labored that he had to have a break. He was weak and weary. It was no longer hard to care for him and to manage Mom's care. He was a more humble man and a more emotional man. I asked him about two days before he died what he would want people to know about his relationship with Jesus. Dad said, "Tell them that there were many times that I let Jesus down, but HE never let me go." Not too long after this conversation, Dad went home to be with Jesus who had not let him go, on February 23, 2023.

What would I have done differently if I had a chance to? Nothing except to be more honest with my dad about my feelings in person. He was not an easy man and came up against me when I was not able to meet his expectations, but I am thankful to have seen a difference at the end of his life. He could not understand that I could spend time being with my family on a good day but would not use that good day to help him. Many of you are in this sandwich generation and know exactly what I am talking about.

Time stood still during this time of hospice. After Dad's death, we took Mom into our home as well as her caregiving for just a month. We had hoped that we would get to see a difference in Mom since she was no longer under Dad's control, but he had been her caregiver by this time for many years. She loved him the most. Mom had a very peaceful home going on March 20, 2023.

My relationship with my dad was always strained, even though he did not see it that way. I wish I had talked more and let him into my life, but I feared the controversy I would stir up if I brought up my own truths to him, just like what had happened when I wrote the letter. I was seeking to live in God's grace and not by the law anymore. I tried not to police his every move and had attempted on other occasions to be honest with him, but he would go into defensive mode every time. I wish I could say that I miss him, and I hope to say that one day. I only miss the father that I had when I was younger and the idea of an unselfish father; the father who was approachable and fun to be with. There were just too many secrets in our family, and I wish that had been different all around.

I struggled with thoughts of Dad's being in heaven, because of his constant anger toward everything and everybody. I was the executor of his and Mom's estate (which is a whole other story), and it was very difficult.

Dad had been the founder and director of a mission board which he used to train pastors and missionaries overseas and to plant churches. I saw Dad's impatience toward the pastors and what I looked at as a lack of love which I thought I should not see in someone called to minister. I am not the judge of his heart; God is.

Dad was a wise businessman, but he did not have a well thought-out plan that would work for the ministry overseas to continue. This was my first point of service as an executor of the estate, to make sure that the missionaries were getting their monthly checks. He refused to put money into the account that would pay the missionaries since he wanted to make sure that Mom's care was taken care of before anything else. There is a whole back story here as to how they were supported by the rents coming in from a building Dad owned. This rental account was frozen and could not be used until after the sale of a commercial building. This took some time. The board voted that the mission would have to shut down as there was nothing in writing that would cover the ministry needs. So, I now had a charitable 501(c)(3) to shut down. It was a lot more than I wanted to do in my neurological condition but one in which I trudged through to completion. It was at the beginning of his estate work that I had this dream that I was talking to Dad. It went like this:

Dad: *Hi Marty.*

Me: *Hi Dad!*

Dad: *I'm sorry that I left things such a mess down there.*

Me: *It's okay, Dad. It must be beautiful up there.*

Dad: *Oh, HE is!*

I woke up with tears rolling down my cheeks and never doubted since that he is with the Lord. It was the first time my dad had ever told me he was sorry. I don't know if any of the rest of my siblings ever heard Dad apologize for anything. He was not only taking in the splendor of heaven, but more importantly, was seeing the beauty of Jesus Christ whom he had faithfully served. I needed this new perspective. The pastors overseas spoke very highly of Dad and Mom, and I am glad that they saw my dad that way.

CHAPTER 8

Mama's Shoes (Legacy)

Save thy people, and bless thine inheritance: feed them also, and lift them up for ever.

— Psalm 28:9 (KJV)

What do you say about the shoes your mama walked in? The ones that made her feel more secure for so many years; the ones that made Dad feel more secure when she was wearing them as he guided her along? I forgot that I still had those shoes tucked away in her room that has now been turned back into my office. That caught me off guard today as I sorted through more boxes. I feel close to her here in my office now.

I remember that one night about a week after she moved in with us when I came and tucked her in to keep her warm at 1:15 a.m. It was such a special night as she was so alert and conversing with me like she had not done in so very long, more than a year ago by that time. That weak little voice that had such little strength was happy that night. I asked her if she wanted me to sleep with her that night. that night that she really understood that her husband of fifty-nine years was with Jesus. She said, "Uh-huh," and we laughed because I found a pair of her pajamas and put them on. As I lay on the day bed next to her hospital bed, I contemplated whether I should have told Mom and hospice said, "By all means, she needs you to be honest with her."

But it was that night that I realized how very tired Mama was. She had walked so long in those shoes, even when we thought she perhaps should already be in a wheelchair. I remember when I was younger, Mama used to love to wear pretty shoes. All of those have long been gone. I will keep one of these pair tucked under the edge of the daybed where I can see them and remember her strength during hard times, her running with her grandchildren, her slowly walking and perhaps running to chop off the heads of snakes that threatened her children and grandchildren; the woman that stood many hours in the kitchen and at the ironing board, and journeyed around the world with her husband sharing the love and joy of Jesus. This woman, who through God's strength beat lymphoma three times, broke her leg in so many places and had a post put in it, wanted it removed, and had to have it put back in, and never walked the same again. What a woman of strength.

She had the same tenacity in her walk with the Lord. She loved Jesus more than life itself and wanted others to know Him and to love Him. She walked in joy where not many could, not without a broken heart at times, but in the power given to her by God's spirit residing in her life. Not many would have kept going, but Mama did. Later in her life, Dad would talk about some dark days she had, but that was not something that she shared with anyone but her beloved husband and with Christ her Savior. I don't remember Mom putting those feet up much until about the last six or seven years when she just couldn't continue very easily. I miss seeing those feet with these shoes propped up in her reclining chair. "Who can find a virtuous woman? for her price is far above rubies" (Proverbs 31:10, KJV). God has my virtuous woman of a mother right there with His Son where she is singing and praising Him all day long.

Oh, Mama, thank you for your love. Thank you for your walk. That walk that is now completely restored, dancing on streets of gold. Mama could "cut a rug." She used to square dance, and at other times, she and Dad would dance beautifully together. I wish I had a glimpse of them in heaven right now, dancing on streets of gold.

When my mama was diagnosed with dementia (later full-blown Alzheimer's disease) twelve years before she went to heaven, we began singing with each other. It was a way I could bring her joy, and it would soothe our heavy hearts. Singing songs with Mama was my delight when I was able to care for her. When my strength returned and I was able to safely give Mom a shower, a song was exactly what she needed to be able to rest easy in the showering process. I miss giving her showers, as it was a time when I know that she trusted me to care for her the most. It was a surprise to all of us how Mama remembered every word of the songs right up until about a month before she crossed that peaceful river into glory. Bible verses were just as familiar to her, and we would recite those as well so that she was hearing the Word. But music was her favorite. That remembrance for her would not have been possible had she not practiced these things earlier in her life.

Dad was sure to lead Mom in Bible reading and prayer up until about two months before he passed, along with choosing a hymn out of their hymn book which sat next to the Bible in order to sing together afterward. We saw this, and it gave us peace to know that no matter how hard the rest of life was, Dad was washing Mom with the water of the Word, and in essence, was keeping her mind holy. Mama no longer sang much during her last few months on Earth as we watched her ability to speak go away, but she always enjoyed the music. I wish I could share with you the songs that we sang together but would be infringing on copyright laws to do so. If you would like to know the songs that gave her the most comfort, you can reach out to me through my website at www.outofthe-woodsbyfaith.com.

What kind of legacy are you leaving? Are you leaving this legacy for the glory of God or only for the people in your life? Is Christ important enough to you to spend time hearing from Him in reading Scripture? Or is this a one-way relationship where you are only praying? Prayer is important, but hearing from God through His Word is most important.

CHAPTER 9

Take Me to the Temple (Missing Out on Life)

Hear the voice of my pleas for mercy, when I cry to you for help, when I lift up my hands toward your most holy sanctuary.

— Psalm 28:2 (ESV)

While my chronic illness was at its worst (about three and a half years ago), I was not able to attend church for the longest time. When I went, the beautiful noise of the service would send me into a seizure. So, I would watch church on Zoom in the safety of my own home where I could have seizures safely (and without humiliation). Everyone was so loving at church to make sure I was okay and to take me to doctor appointments, to help with meals at times they were needed, and to just be there for me and my husband. We are so blessed by our church and thank God for her! I longed to be with the people worshipping with them, when God gave me this poem/one-day song based on Jonah 2.

Take Me to the Temple

Take me to the Temple.
Take me to the Tabernacle of Praise.

It only takes a moment to look around.
  Instead of looking up, to Your glorious face, I find myself spiraling downward.
  Then, I am weary in this race
  I can believe the lie that I've lost my place.
  Help me look up, help me look in Your Word for truth to steer me onward.

Back up to the Temple
Back up to the Tabernacle of Praise

You have afflicted me in my mind and the enemy would seek to bring shame and disgrace, and I find myself spiraling downward.
  I ask you to cast down these idols that rise up in my heart when its seaweed would squeeze me out. They are so worthless, forsaking Your mercy. I am so weak, and I need You to…

Bring me to Your Temple.
Bring me to Your Tabernacle of Praise.

You have brought up my life from the depths of despair … where my soul nearly fainted, with no strength to care, and I find myself looking upward.

I come to sacrifice to You, with thanksgiving in my heart.

Salvation comes only from You.

In Your glory I share no part … and I'm

Going to Your Temple
Going to Your Tabernacle of Praise.

This Temple is Your Spirit, brought down from my Father above, falling so tenderly on Your fearful little bird, looking here and looking there.

My eyes see You in Your Word.

The noise continues in my head, but You are there and faithful to…

Take me to Your Temple.
Take me to Your Tabernacle of Praise.

How could I start this time so strong in faith, and soon descend to the depths?

I am undone by Your gracious longsuffering for Your daughter!

Your love reaches so deep in my soul, so deep into Your Temple, and You squeeze out praise. You extend Your branch of love for me to land on, so I have…

Safety in Your Temple.
Safety in Your Tabernacle of Praise.

Blessed Savior, You are my hiding place, and I long to rest in Your care where nothing else matters except that You are here.

Take me to Your Temple
Take me to Your Tabernacle of Praise.

— Marcia Escobar
April 16, 2020

This was written after a month and a half of sickness (beginning March 1, 2020), displacement from March 2, 2020, tornado damage, and the beginning of quarantine for coronavirus pandemic. And You are Good. You are Holy. You are ever-present, sovereign, and in control!

CHAPTER 10

Living by Faith in the "In-Between" of Chronic Illness

> *I am crucified with Christ: nevertheless I live; yet not I, but Christ liveth in me: and the life which I now live in the flesh I live by the faith of the Son of God, who loved me, and gave himself for me.*
>
> — Galatians 2:20 (KJV)

There is this beautiful and painful in-between space in life called daily living. It is the joy that we have when we get to be with our kids and grandkids. There is the joy that awaits the dying saint as their body prepares to go home to be with the Lord (like Dad awaited in 2023 for twenty-four days on hospice and my sweet mama waited for another twenty-five days after that to experience).

Then smashed in between that joy with loved ones and grief experienced in the death of both of my parents in such a shockingly short time for me is suffering with health issues that I wonder if I will live with for the rest of my life. I have, to date, lost 70 percent of my hearing in my right ear with Meniere's disease, and at any time, dizziness can rear its ugly head and put me in bed or at the side of a toilet with nausea.

Will I suffer well? Will I be okay? Will there be a cure on this side of glory for this disease? My heart longs for it, but more than that, I long to have some great parts in between the suffering where God allows me to be used to magnify Him in the lives of others and to enjoy a full day.

I wish you could see some of the joyful and painful in-betweens in my life as they have been glorious. The spinning and nauseousness of my vertigo from Meniere's disease and shuffling around without being able to see to get to bed while my dear husband so gently guides me and lets me stop to rest my weary head on his shoulder and cry on the way there, you will not see. But it is where my in-between is for now. I am living and want to live and that's a huge blessing. I am living and longing to trust completely that God makes no mistakes and does all things well. I pray for faith and blessings and joy in between it all.

> *Lord, help me in each in-between of life's stages to thank You and to praise You. This life is not about me or any other person, and ever since the garden of Eden, it is about God calling the world back to a relationship with Himself. Period. What a wasted life to think that we even exist for any other reason. Lord, I believe. Help me to cherish the joyful in-between parts and to keep believing and trusting when the in-between is like a bologna, peanut butter, and radish sandwich. As a middle schooler this used to be my favorite. This sandwich no longer is my favorite and it sounds gross now. The point is, Father, help me to be faithful to love You and to pray for others who may or may not*

believe in You, to comfort with the comfort You have given to me, and to have joy in this dizzy journey. I love You, Lord.

Where are you at in your heart during the in-betweens? Do you shake your angry fist at your Creator God? Do you feel like He owes you something for the times you were able to serve Him faithfully? Do you really believe that He is in control and is the Lord of the outcomes? Stop fighting and surrender to Him, seeking joy for the journey in His Word.

CHAPTER 11

Running Knees— the Power of God's Word and Prayer

For whatsoever things were written aforetime were written for our learning, that we through patience and comfort of the scriptures might have hope.

— Romans 15:4 (KJV)

Romans 15:4 is the verse that my then biblical counselor, now pastor, emailed to me when we were making our trip to Tennessee to get a fresh start and to seek biblical soul care after infidelity invaded our marriage and family. Without this type of counseling, I believe my marriage would have ended in divorce, and the enemy would have won. God saw fit to save our marriage. This was the hardest struggle of our lives, but it was worth it to fight for our marriage. This passage of Scripture was what I needed to get me set on the right path of God's Word being completely and fully sufficient for everything we would need to fight this battle of divorce and to walk in newness of life and to have hope.

It was a few years later that I wrote this prayer and struggle for guidance. Yes, it has been a long journey back from betrayal. It has been worth it all (although not wished on anyone except to see the cross) for the joy in our lives that Christ has formed in our hearts through the breastplate of righteousness that He formed by my husband's and my obedience.

My Prayer

Father,

You have me here on my knees, on my face, surrounded by Your ceaseless grace, and yet, I struggle. I struggle with a belief system that is tainted by this world's system. One which would have me try to bring myself above this mess; one which would have me take this pill … it will make you feel better, one which would state that you can't just let people walk all over you. Why would I be drawn to anyone or anything but You to help me with this situation? Why would I think I have the power to lift myself above the things that You ordain for my life?

Jesus, You are the absolute picture of humility, and You allowed people to despise You, spit on You, slap You, hate You, use You for Your healing power with no thought of continuing to live in gratitude for this healing You gave. We gloss over this well-known passage but listen to its implications for our lives as we think that we should not have to bear up under suffering … that we should have the last word. Are we better than Jesus Christ?

He is despised and rejected by men,
A Man of sorrows and acquainted with grief.

And we hid, as it were, our faces from Him;
He was despised, and we did not esteem Him.
Surely, He has borne our griefs
And carried our sorrows;
Yet we esteemed Him stricken,
Smitten by God, and afflicted.
But He was wounded for our transgressions,
He was bruised for our iniquities;
The chastisement for our peace was upon Him,
And by His stripes we are healed.
All we like sheep have gone astray;
We have turned, everyone, to his own way;
And the LORD has laid on Him the iniquity of us all.
He was oppressed, and He was afflicted,
Yet He opened not His mouth;
He was led as a lamb to the slaughter,
And as a sheep before its shearers is silent,
So He opened not His mouth.
He was taken from prison and from judgment,
And who will declare His generation?
For He was cut off from the land of the living;
For the transgressions of My people He was stricken.
And they made His grave with the wicked—
But with the rich at His death,
Because He had done no violence,
Nor was any deceit in His mouth.
Yet it pleased the LORD to bruise Him;
He has put Him to grief.
When You make His soul an offering for sin,
He shall see His seed, He shall prolong His days,

And the pleasure of the LORD shall prosper in His hand.
He shall see the labor of His soul and be satisfied.
By His knowledge My righteous Servant shall justify many,
For He shall bear their iniquities.
Therefore I will divide Him a portion with the great,
And He shall divide the spoil with the strong,
Because He poured out His soul unto death,
And He was numbered with the transgressors,
And He bore the sin of many,
And made intercession for the transgressors.

— Isaiah 53:3–12 (NKJV)

Why would I think that I have the power in myself alone to bring myself above all the situations of my life? It's because my belief system is messed up. It's because, at the end of the day, as much as I want to trust God with every aspect of my life, I think that it is somehow within me to help God. *Wow, how proud is that?* For me to think that my almighty Creator, Savior, Sustainer needs my help. He saved me from the wretched sin in my life, gives me the same power in my life that raised His Son from the grave, has given me everything that I need for life and godliness in His Word, and I think I should have a better plan? Hear it from Peter in the inspired Word of God:

> *Grace and peace be multiplied to you in the knowledge of God and of Jesus our Lord, as His divine power has given to us all things that pertain to life and godliness, through the knowledge of Him who called us by glory*

> *and virtue, by which have been given to us exceedingly great and precious promises, that through these you may be partakers of the divine nature, having escaped the corruption that is in the world through lust.*
>
> — 2 Peter 1:2–4 (NKJV)

There is an enemy of all our souls that would have us believe a lie, that there is salvation in ourselves, in a substance, in a doctor, in anything but Jesus. It's as old as the garden, but we still succumb to the lies of Satan. Listen to Peter as he addressed the Sanhedrin and the high priests and rulers of their time as they came up against him and John as they preached Christ alone for salvation and healing, regardless of the day of the week. This should be the theme of all our lives … *nor is there salvation in any other.*

> *Then Peter, filled with the Holy Spirit, said to them, "Rulers of the people and elders of Israel: If we this day are judged for a good deed done to a helpless man, by what means he has been made well, let it be known to you all, and to all the people of Israel, that by the name of Jesus Christ of Nazareth, whom you crucified, whom God raised from the dead, by Him this man stands here before you whole. This is the 'stone which was rejected by you builders, which has become the chief cornerstone.' Nor is there salvation in any other, for there is no other name under heaven given among men by which we must be saved."*
>
> — Acts 4:8–12 (NKJV)

Today, dear Lord, as I meditate on You and Your power and direction for my life, I pray that You will help me to "lay aside every weight, and the sin which so easily ensnares *us*, and let us run with endurance the race that is set before us, looking unto Jesus, the author and finisher of our faith" (Hebrews 12:1–2, NKJV). Your will for my life is so clearly outlined in Scripture. Help me to always go there for guidance. Help me to be on my knees both literally and in spirit as in 1 Thessalonians 5:16–18 (NKJV), "Rejoice always, pray without ceasing, give thanks in all circumstances; for this is the will of God in Christ Jesus for you."

> *For this cause I bow my knees unto the Father of our Lord Jesus Christ*
> *Of whom the whole family in heaven and earth is named,*
> *That he would grant you, according to the riches of his glory, to be strengthened with might by his Spirit in the inner man;*
> *That Christ may dwell in your hearts by faith; that ye, being rooted and grounded in love,*
> *May be able to comprehend with all saints what is the breadth, and length, and depth, and height;*
> *And to know the love of Christ, which passeth knowledge, that ye might be filled with all the fulness of God.*
>
> — Ephesians 3:14–19 (KJV)

Is God truly enough for you? For me? Will we be content to rest in His goodness and grace even if we are never healed? Will you love Him even if everyone leaves you?

CHAPTER 12

Running Knees— Intercession (Letting People In)

God is our refuge and strength, a very present help in trouble.

— Psalm 46:1 (ESV)

And there she came, running on her knees, to bring me to our Father's throne.

The countless people whom she has brought to this place are to be left unknown.

A woman to be trusted as she lets our requests be known to the One she lovingly fears.

It doesn't matter if the answer does not come in a day, in months, or in years…

she still runs.

She cares deeply and loves the same.

In her conversation, she blesses Your holy name.

An example of Christ she is to so many, and I count her as a cherished friend,

one to love and treasure to the end.

A virtuous woman, who can find? I praise You, Father that I see You in my Jane.

Your precious blood flows through her veins!
The work on this Earth is not complete in her life, and she rests in You as her guide.
To follow You, she knows is best, and it brings her rest when in Your Word she abides.

God is in the midst of her; she shall not be moved; God will help her when morning dawns.

— Psalm 46:5

Strength and dignity are her clothing, and she laughs at the time to come.

— Proverbs 31:25

Do you have a friend who will lift you up in prayer? Will you be humble enough and vulnerable enough to seek out this person, whom you need in your life, who is not afraid to let you know that they are praying for you? Who is not afraid to pray for you at the moment the need is mentioned? I dare you to pray that God brings this person into your life. Know this: they are not your Savior, but they are willing to take your needs to their Savior. I am blessed by my friend, Jane, that she is this kind of friend to me. I long to be this kind of friend to others in order to bring God glory.

CHAPTER 13

Finding Hearts Everywhere (Looking with Spirit Eyes)

Having the eyes of your hearts enlightened, that you may know what is the hope to which he has called you, what are the riches of his glorious inheritance in the saints.

— Ephesians 1:18

My dear friend, Kay, sees hearts in so many places and shows us so many unique places all the time in which she sees them. I have concluded that the reason Kay is seeing hearts in everything is because she looks for them. It has become a habit and a good one. Even when she doesn't truly look for hearts, they come about in the oddest places at times.

The thought occurred to me that we can go through our lives as believers completely missing the joy of our salvation, resisting God at every turn and complaining about the simplest or even most difficult circumstances that happen that is not according to how we think it should go in our expectations (pre-planned disappointments). The change is made when we are renewed in our minds through God's Word (Romans 12:2) and seek the things of God (Matthew 6:33), recognizing that

His divine power gives us all things that pertain to life and godliness (2 Peter 1:3). Open the eyes of our heart, Lord, so that we may see with Your Spirit eyes and not miss what You have for each moment. Searching for Him with all our hearts is a life worth pursuing. God's promise to Israel still applies to us today. "You will seek me and find me, when you seek me with all your heart" (Jeremiah 29:13, ESV).

Kay, I love that you are allowed and choose to see hearts in everything! You inspire me!

As being someone who grew up with negativity and without a voice, it has been hard for me to see the best in every person and every circumstance. How about you? Are you discontent? Do you let life's trials send you into a downward spiral at every turn? Are you thankful? Will you CHOOSE to look for the good and let God have His glory in your trials?

CHAPTER 14

Becoming Sparkly (Where Do You Find Comfort?)

Be thou my strong habitation, whereunto I may continually resort: thou hast given commandment to save me; for thou art my rock and my fortress

— Psalm 71:3 (KJV)

Jesus, You are the brightness of God's glory.
And because of Your sacrifice,
We are able to have the same shiny image.
But, God, You gave us each a story.
A story where we choose who goes with us on this pilgrimage.

Today, will I allow You to walk with me
To help me in the choices of the day?
Or will I first choose to pick up the phone and flee
Into conversation with a friend?
To hear what they have to say?

*Will Your Word be my first choice
Of comfort, shaping my behavior?
Or will I listen to another voice,
Turning to some other false god
To be my savior?*

*Father, help me to let You have Your way,
And on You my selfish desires to lay.
Thank You that yesterday is past,
And thanks that today You give me a whole new day
To change the chapters of my story.*

*Today I invite You to trod this path with me
So I will come out sparkling
In the light of Your glory.*

Milton Keynes UK
Ingram Content Group UK Ltd.
UKHW010235111224
452348UK00011B/775